Living
Intuitively

Living Intuitively

Reaping Life's Rich Benefits

BRUCE WAY

CELESTIAL ARTS
BERKELEY, CA

Celestial Arts
P.O. Box 7123
Berkeley, California 94707

Distributed in Canada by Publishers Group West, in the United
Kingdom and Europe by Airlift Books, in Singapore and Malaysia
by Berkeley Books, and in South Africa by Real Books.

Originally published in Australia by Lothian Books

Cover design by Fifth Street Design
Interior design by Stanley Wong

Library of Congress Cataloging-in-Publication Data

Way, Bruce
    Living intuitively: reaping life's rich benefits / by Bruce Way.
        p.   cm.
    Includes bibliographical references (p.   ) and index.
    ISBN 0-89087-845-5 (pbk.)
        1. Intuition (Psychology) 2. Self-actualization (Psychology)
I. Title.
BF315.5.W39 1997
153.4'4--dc21   97-38928
                                                   CIP

Printed in the United States

1 2 3 4 5 6 - 00 99 98 97

Contents

Author's Note 7

Introduction 11

1 *Educating the Ego* 17

WINTER

2 *A Time to Release the Past* 29

3 *First Clear the Water* 43

4 *Keeping the Pool Clear* 61

5 *Oh! Just Before You Climb the Ladder* 75

SPRING

6 *A Time to Grow Your Intuition* 85

7 *Let's Do Some Warm-up Exercises* 89

8 *Intuitive Playtime* 103

9 *Practise, Practise, Practise* 113

SUMMER

10 *A Time of Endurance* 121

11 *Be Excited by the Experience* 127

12 *Perfecting Your Style* 135

13 *After Perfection — What Then?* 141

AUTUMN

14 *A Time to Reap Rewards* 149

15 *In Search of a Higher Platform* 159

16 *Questions and Answers* 163

Index 169

Further Reading 173

Dedication

Katrina,
May the winds of love forever whisper through your hair
May the flames of inspiration dance around your feet
May the earth's power strengthen your creativity
May the waters of life vitalise your sensitivity
And may that horse, adorned in red, carry you safely across the universe, forever.

Acknowledgements

Ken Harry, whose understanding, wisdom and great love for the intuitive lifestyle set me on the path, kept my feet on it and inspired me to accept it for myself.

Jan Greenfield, whose compassion and Virgoan realism, showed me the foundation of living intuitively and taught me how to use it in this world unselfishly.

Jacqueline Simcox, whose wisdom, friendship and un-wavering belief in my quest, taught me that life just is forever,

I thank you.

AUTHOR'S NOTE

Several years ago I stumbled across my intuition and realised that my life became richer every time I used it. It started for me when I felt that I wanted to write. I secretly bought a diary and began writing my intuitively inspired thoughts. Sometimes it took a minute and sometimes hours. At first, because I was so excited by the process, I would re-read my notes as soon as I had finished writing. However, the content made little sense to me and because of that my enthusiasm would wane. Yet something continued to drive me and I began to leave the material unread. I recognised that I needed time to adjust because these intuitions were not my usual way of thinking. Eventually, I went over my notes and was astounded at the common sense advice in front of me.

Intuition is inherent in everyone. Some call it a hunch and others a gut feeling. It is that flash of creative brilliance that seems to come out of nowhere when we least expect it. Because intuitive thought is different from the way we are taught to think in school we need a different approach to learn how to use it. Most people who don't have the opportunity to be taught by another intuitive person, develop intuitively by daring to follow a hunch. The hunch works out and the person is encouraged to try it again and again and again until it just becomes second nature. Most intuitives that I know have learnt by this trial and error approach. I was no exception. I didn't understand my intuition at first. It was just a series of unsubstantiated hunches. Yet I began to listen to them and follow them one at a time. When a hunch worked out I was encouraged to try the next one. When one didn't, I focused on the last successful hunch and kept going anyway.

Although my intuition continually pushed me to write, it seemed intellectually preposterous. All that I had written in my life were school and university assignments and sales proposals. While my head vehemently debated the issues, my heart was writing poetry. So write I would whenever the intuitive thoughts stirred within.

I wanted to write and teach people how to live intuitively although, when you consider my background, that thought was quite irrational. I was raised in a conservative Christian family, attended church regularly and believed that inspiration either came from God or the Devil — certainly not from me. If the inspired thought was in keeping with the church's teachings then it was from God. If it didn't . . . well to put it another way, I had better not think about it. To think that my intuition could teach me was absurd. So I based most of my decisions on intellectual reason that was corroborated by my elders.

There is a rebellious streak in me, however, matched by an insatiable thirst for knowledge. Therefore while telling myself that I was crazy I nevertheless wanted to find someone who could teach me to listen to my intuition. I soon learnt that when we need answers our intuition will quickly provide them. On a hunch I went to see a colleague thinking that she might know of someone. We chatted in her office for about fifteen minutes before she stopped, looked at me with an impish grin, and said that she had nothing else to say. I was so confused that I looked down at some questions I'd previously written in my notebook and realised that she had answered all but the last one. To my amazement she had answered all these questions without me having asked them!

I asked her how she knew and she grinned again saying that she just had a hunch. This was my moment. No matter how crazy I thought I was to want to become intuitive I had to ask her the final question. So, nervously, and almost choking on my words, I asked her if she knew of anyone who could teach me. She settled back into her chair and beamed. It seemed, coincidentally, that she did and she gave me the telephone number of Jan, my first teacher.

I continued to work in the computer industry while I developed my intuition. Yes, I kept my day job and the corporate arena proved to be the ideal playground for my conscious intuitive development. Here I could apply the lessons to the realities of daily life, practise them and observe the results. *Living Intuitively — Reaping Life's Rich Benefits* is what I learnt during this period of my life.

Today, I am an author, consultant and keynote speaker. I teach people how to benefit daily by living intuitively. Intuitive thought is different from other types of thinking. Intuition is a feeling that translates into words often with a more poetic turn of phrase. Therefore, I have placed in italics some direct intuitive texts to show you intuition at work. These passages are verbatim transcripts. I have included them to show you the poetry in creative expression, which is an integral part of our lives and a sign that intuition is at work.

Living Intuitively — Reaping Life's Rich Benefits was born from an intuition. It represents several years of study and personal experimentation. Just as many before us have discovered the benefits of living intuitively so will you. By living intuitively you will find your creative core and teach yourself how to find the riches of life.

Introduction

TRY TO IMAGINE a space that is infinitely multi-dimensional. It has innumerable layers, contours, and depth. Now put into this space all the people that you know. Include everyone from your closest friends to people whom you've never met although have heard about. Next put into this multi-dimensional space all the people that you become aware of by watching television, listening to the radio, reading books, newspapers or whom you see as you go about your daily business. Do you agree that the picture is beginning to look like an insurance company's prospect list? We haven't finished yet. Try to imagine all those people standing quite still and connect them by a single infinitely expandable thread.

Understanding the dynamics of interpersonal relationships is a relatively simple task while the circumstances remain the same. But what happens, when all these people begin to move in any direction at once across every dimension of this multi-dimensional space? Think about it and try to visualise the scene that would follow. Perhaps from our privileged observation post, we might see an eternally growing entanglement of inter-personal links that quickly becomes indecipherable.

This model constantly changes each time a person enters the space. Each new arrival connects to the single thread in a way that is perpetually consistent. Think about the multiplicity of thoughts, actions and results that are forever weaving patterns into this intricate web of life. I imagine that, if we could see the interconnections of life, they would look like a tangled ball of wool after a playful kitten had finished with it.

LINEAR THINKING

In their rush to find the answers of life, people try to understand its process by isolating specific behavioural aspects and then dissecting them. The results of such exploration are fixed laws that are, among other things, used to predict future events or outcomes. After we mould our thoughts this way we tend to fight to prevent them from changing, even though reality changes. I call this thinking linear — and it can be best explained by the idea of cause and effect. That is, a particular cause will, predictably, have a certain effect. This type of thinking binds us to the past because it assumes that particular actions always produce the same results.

Attempting to tie the ball of wool on to a linear framework is analogous to the chicken and egg conundrum. It can be frustrating because, to analyse linearly, we must first establish a solid reference point. But where is the start of the thread? Or which is the cause and which the effect; Perhaps the effect of the cause is the cause of the new effect; we can go on ad infinitum. I suggest that this is the intellectual thought process of the linear personality.

Linear thinking always seeks reasons to explain outcomes according to past events. The notion of tradition, for example, is essentially linear in character. 'We must do it this way because we always have and it has always proved successful' is a common catchcry of people when they lose the courage to continue exploring and to create. When linear thinking people look at the ball of wool they see a tangled mess because they are constantly trying to find the beginning and the end of it. Yet what looks tangled to them is actually an intricate interconnection of possibilities and opportunities. To try to understand the ball of wool intellectually is confusing. To understand it intuitively is enlightening.

MULTI-DIMENSIONAL (INTUITIVE) THINKING

Did you notice the difference in the last two sentences in the paragraph above? When we take out the word 'try', understanding becomes effortless. Similarly, intuitive thinking is effortless. It is characterised by a sense of knowing. It is a feeling and as such provides us with a hint on how it functions. Intuition is the language of the soul. It is the quiet, calming voice that always speaks to us when we are ready to listen to it.

When we view the ball of wool as a whole, then we know that the relationships it represents can grow and change in any way at all. This thinking is multi-dimensional; it does not involve causal relationships because it is whole in itself, irrespective of shape or form. The ball of wool has no past and no future because it is whole in every moment. When it chooses to change a part of itself it creates a new present or a new now. This is the nature of our soul. The soul has many definitions and connotations. In this text I refer to the soul as our creative essence. Our creativity can move away from the linear idea of cause and effect and into multi-dimensional thought. I will define both states of thought in more detail later in the text. Both modalities of thought are valid. To tap into our creative source we use our intuition so that we can access our soul, talk to it and bring it into creative form in our lives.

INTUITION — THE LANGUAGE OF THE SOUL

Intuition is the language of the soul. When our soul speaks to us, it does so intuitively. It sends out an intuitive thought to our conscious self. We hear the message through our feelings and translate it into the conscious intelligence of the mind. Intuition is a part of our soul and is not constrained by the consequences predicted by linear thought. In other words, it is via the soul that we create the opportunities necessary for our development and manifest tangible benefits, in linear terms, in our lives.

THE ILLUSION OF LOSS

All too often we become obsessed with finding the start of something that happened in another time that has no relevance to the present situation. Ask yourself how your life would benefit if you found the start of the woollen thread. Perhaps we passionately search for our roots because we are afraid to move forward and grow in this moment! Do we, by searching into our past, turn our backs on the rich opportunities that are right before our eyes and attainable now?

Notice those people who try to control others and recognise their game. Witness how they bring up the past to deny the future and how they build the illusion of loss in an attempt to keep us from reaping life's rich benefits. This is why the notion of death or loss is absent in the following chapters.

Fear of death slows the experiential process of learning that feeds our prosperity. It's important for us to experience many situations so that we can learn. Therefore we require constant change from one experience to another. The ego is charged with our survival. It causes us to resist anything that may contribute to our death. Now if we think in a linear way then we program the ego, by creating the illusion of loss, to fight the notion of change and hold on at all costs. The price we pay for this is conflict and control that typically express themselves outwardly as the wars of humankind. The personal price we pay for holding on is disease on the mental, emotional and physical levels of our beings.

In reality, there is nothing we experience that we lose. Each experience simply integrates into the knowledge banks hidden in the ball of wool and transforms into wisdom for our future benefit. Experience is the essence of life and for change to take place we must let go of the dogma of death. When we believe that death is the end of the line and is the termination of all things that preceded it, then we block ourselves from expressing our creativity. What we create however is the linear belief of fear.

I attended a lecture once where the lecturer defined fear as False Expectations Appearing Real and I can't think of a better way to describe it. Energy merely changes form and because all matter is energy the death of anything is an impossibility. There is no finality to our existence yet when those who foster the notion of finality apply it, they always create the illusion of fear. Fear is insidious, especially when those who have mastered their fears realise that they can control others by using the belief of permanent loss as a weapon to force their will onto others.

THE RICHNESS OF EXPERIENCE

We create experiences in our lives to learn from them. They are necessary because they teach us to realise that we are infinitely creative. However, when we process information generated by linear thought then we are motivated to act in ways to avoid change and hence avoid loss. When we think multi-dimen-sionally, we re-program the ego to release its attachment to the past and to create from a position of endless opportunity.

The sensation of pain plays a vital role in telling us the nature of our thinking. Now we can learn. We use our innate intelli-gence to instruct the ego and re-program it if required. This is how thought creates reality. Personal responsibility then takes on more meaning when we recognise that we are completely in charge of our life's processes in every moment. Give the ideas of fear and loss no importance and allow the illusions to dissolve effortlessly. As these illusions disperse and you con-nect into the loving guidance of the soul, your life will balance of its own accord manifesting peace, harmony, continual growth and prosperity.

All too often we hear concerned action groups wanting to save this or that. Yet when we look behind their actions we often find politically motivated power games to force in more rules by inducing the fear that something we love or revere will die and be lost forever. It is the fear of loss that motivates humankind to obsessively hold onto the past.

One certainty of life is, that I am who I am because I am and because I am, I am one hundred per cent responsible for my happiness, prosperity and environment. The fundamental choice that we all have is whether we chose to listen to our intuition and allow it to express itself in our lives or to live in restrictive linear thought.

To learn the language of the soul and to live intuitively can seem confronting at first because we need to convince our-selves of the validity of creative expression and let go of our linear beliefs about loss and the avoidance of pain. I guarantee that, once you have listened to your intuition and used it to create prosperously, living intuitively will be as effortless as a peaceful walk in the park.

Living intuitively is exciting, stimulating and rewarding. People who live intuitively undoubtedly create harmonious prosperity on all levels of their beings. When you allow this 'soul' prosperity to manifest in your life, your prosperity will also flow to anyone with whom you associate. Your creative essence is so powerful that once you can consciously com-municate with it you will discover that intuition has been at work in your life even before you knew of its existence! Why?

Because intuition has always been with you to teach you how to create. You are your creator. You are perfectly connected to the universal source of creativity which some call God. Your intuitive expression is unique to you, it is with you right now and is waiting for you to extend your hand to it, in love and use it.

1

Educating the Ego

You are your best teacher. Implanted in your life are the lessons of growth. The Halls of Learning are where you live. So learn from your experiences and reflect on who you are. Learn and experience the value of personal responsibility by living in this moment and making choices freely. This is, after all, the basis of living intuitively.

THE INTUITIVE PERSON is forever seeking out soul-to-soul communications. Indeed all people are intuitive. The only difference between those who act on their intuitions and those who don't is a matter of belief. We are the product of our upbringing and the way we perceived the values, beliefs and attitudes of the communities in which we lived as children. This state of controlled reactive behaviour remains with us until we consciously look at our patterns and choose to accept our status quo or change it.

INTUITION DEFINED

Intuition is that innate ability that enables us to access the knowledge that is *in*side of ourselves. This library of knowledge contains all the *tuition* we need to grow and expand. It is, if you like, a part of the soul. Intuition, taken one step further, is the ability to communicate with the soul. Intuition is the language of the soul.

As children, the attitudes of those close to us, such as parents, siblings, aunts and uncles significantly influenced us. Our interactions with them helped shape our willingness to live intuitively or otherwise. Intuition is associated with feelings. It is intangible and traditionally identified as a female trait. As science became more prominent and took more control of our thinking, it cast doubts on the validity of intuition in modern society. Consequently, society can sometimes view intuitives as radicals because intuitive behaviour is not the current standard. Therefore, for those people influenced by social opinion and who need society's acceptance to feed their self-esteem, the ability to intuit is pushed well down into their psyches. It then lies dormant underneath the metres of debris that are products of rational scientific argument. We are all social creatures and in this context, to varying degrees, we take on social conditioning.

In *Living Intuitively* I aim to teach you how to use your intuition to consciously travel between yourself as personality and yourself as soul. Once you master this art you will also know how to communicate with people, soul to soul, and to live in harmony with your environment.

THE ART OF DOING

When I started writing and speaking about intuition, I noticed that my life magically adjusted to the lessons being written and taught — sometimes dramatically and at other times in subtle ways. I lived each article I wrote word by word. By the time I was published, I really thought that I had mastered the art of intuition. Then, as interest grew and the publicity bit, readers began contacting me to say how much they appreciated the message.

'Thank you for the article or lecture' was a common response. 'Because of your words I've changed my life.' These calls encouraged me because I heard people affirming that they were in charge of their lives and going for their dreams. They were doing something! Sure they liked what I said and, from my perspective, that was great. Yet the comment that 'I've changed my life' was, for me, where it was at.

That was exciting!

Then there were others. 'The article is wonderful', they said, 'I agree with everything you say. I couldn't put it down until I finished it', and they would pause before continuing:

'The meditations you describe sound wonderful but I just can't get into them at the moment. Can you put me on your mailing list and when you run the next workshop I will do them then? Oh, by the way I've lent the article to several of my friends who all say that they enjoyed it too.'

Personally I love praise. Yet every time I heard this I had a nagging feeling that just wouldn't go away. For a while it puzzled me until I realised that the second group of people had only accepted my words on an intellectual basis. They told their friends about it and then did nothing themselves. I tallied the responses and as the number grew it became evident that the first response represented about one-fifth of the sample and the second category was by far in the majority.

During this time new challenges presented themselves daily. I began speaking at functions, appearing on radio and television and in the press. These media commitments tested me to the limit. I quickly realised that I had no relevant experience on which to base decisions and limited experience in answering the continual stream of probing questions being put to me. I did understand that intuitive living had innumerable facets to it depending on which person's perspective was in the spotlight at the time. Consequently, I found that it was near impossible to prepare myself for an interview. Intellectually this scared me. Intuitively, however, I knew that no preparation was necessary. Each situation would take care of itself. To demonstrate intuition I had only to talk from the heart and allow the words to come. This was the time when I had to live my truth.

Since that time I've learnt much. I now know that by writing about intuition I started a journey that required me to walk it intuitively. Now I am telling you this for a reason. There are at least two ingredients to successful intuitive living. The first is to understand what it is and to learn all that you can about it. The second is to live it. Intellectual understanding is not enough. Experience is not enough. Experience and knowledge together are the basis on which to learn how to live intuitively. You, as the pupil, are the receiver of information. You, as the teacher, are the doer of the information. To teach yourself you must instruct the pupil to put the books down, leave the safe environment of the intellect, and go outside to live the lessons.

I may be able to write books that have audience appeal but unless you, the reader, determine to put your intuition into action, then your knowledge will remain intellectually based, motionless and inert. The soul is about inspiring the ego into action. It continually prompts you into action so that it can learn and create, create, create. The message for me since beginning this journey is strong and I pass it on as sound counsel. Intellectual expression, no matter how profound, is valueless without activity. We are indeed our best teachers!

Learning takes on many different guises. We can learn by absorbing information through our senses and then formulate intellectual theories. We go to schools, colleges and universities to receive information and intellectually process it. On leaving these institutions we go into the world to apply our lessons and to experience the results of our actions. It's by experiencing in this way that we either accept or reject the validity of our prior reasoning. Intellectual learning takes place in the mind. Experiential learning takes place by doing something. The teaching process then has two components — intellectual and experiential. This is true in any avenue of life. Learning requires thought *and* action. We must do something to consolidate our theories and practise our lessons. In this way we integrate the wisdom gained by living. This 'doing' is the role of the ego.

POSITIONING THE EGO

There are numerous definitions of ego and hence many belief systems about it. All are valid because each relates to the experiences of the person formulating the definition. I see the ego as the driving force of your personality in the world. Your ego motivates you to behave in certain ways which put together form your personality. The ego is the ignition switch to the motor of your personality. Once it ignites your engine, the personality is propelled into the environment, interacts with it and experiences the effects of its actions. Thought is the key to turn the ego on. We instruct the ego through our thoughts from information drawn either from the linear reality of cause and effect or the multi-dimensional reality of unlimited opportunity. The ego then processes the information according to your belief system and guides your personality into action.

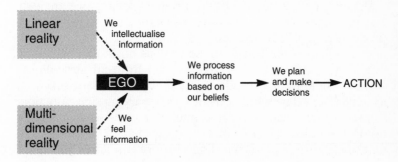

Diagram 1 — The ego filters information which comes from both linear and multi-dimensional reality.

Inactivity occurs when the ego is unsure about the consequence of the action and whether it may have a damaging effect. Ultimately inactivity creates stagnation. The life force or spirit then becomes imprisoned within the confines of inaction and recedes until eventually, unless it reactivates, it stands still.

EGO IN SURVIVAL MODE

Traditionally, we have learnt and acquired skills to dominate others and our environment. It seems that somewhere in our past we decided that domination was the key to survival. We believed that by being more aggressive, stronger and faster, we had the formula for success and that we could only succeed by winning over others. In time, we began to view those around us as either allies or enemies and we developed beliefs based on disparity. Just look at the advertising around us. We are asked to think in terms of better or worse, stronger or weaker, intelligent or ignorant, and life or death. Therefore, for a person to succeed, in this context, someone must win and someone must lose. We project this attitude in our sport. The Olympic Games for example, an arena for athletes to break free of their perceived limitations, has now become a competition of national pride and medal tallies. Such competition is said to benefit our lives and our businesses. This need for aggressive domination shows itself periodically in ideological wars, either religious, economic or just through plain ol' greed. It was and still is the war of humankind.

Because people are the basis of human society, we are also the foundations of organisations and structures established to promote group ideas that strive to achieve the common goals of the individual in the group. So too has business evolved in much the same way. We have moved from an agricultural society where people produced all they required for survival, to the present day, where businesses of varying sizes function to profit the myriad associated interest groups such as shareholders, employees, customers and suppliers. The problem is that one person's understanding of profit can differ considerably from another's. There are as many definitions of profit as there are people on this planet, or so it seems.

We live in a world of large scale and rapid change. With the arrival of the space age, computer technology and sophisticated communications techniques, the world moves much faster than it has ever done before. The need for leaders at all levels to be able to make decisions faster and more accurately, to generate ideas and implement them effectively with shorter and shorter lead times is becoming more crucial for the success of any venture. Governments and their structures appear unable to cater for rapid change effectively and the same happens in corporations and business.

I remember speaking to a senior executive who estimated that it took at least eight years to change a company's culture, attitudes and direction. The problem that we all face today is that change happens a lot faster than eight years. Can you remember the days of the ten-year plan? When this became inadequate we built in different time range plans. I am sure there are plenty of readers who will agree that three years is now a millennium away when you're trying to predict market direction and future trends. So how do we forward plan for our businesses? How do we gear production facilities for rapid change? How do we determine the lifecycle of products or services and how do we plan our own lives to achieve complete prosperity as we define it, experience it and live it?

When we look at history, which can be the moment of time just passed or thousands of years ago, humans always seem to have one fundamental choice to make. Do we run our lives, our businesses, our relationships, our games and our world on the premise of war and fight to succeed over human and social casualties or do we choose another method? Do we have the courage to talk to our soul and find out how we can generate ideas more quickly, more simply and more effectively? Intuitive communication with the soul is the hallmark of the new leader. This person will allow her or his soul to increase prosperity across all facets of life and will apply their intuitive skill to society, business, government and other arenas of interest for greater prosperity.

EGO AS AN EXPRESSION OF SOUL

In *Living Intuitively* I will introduce you to these skills and show you how to develop your own special brand of intuition. Please understand that you have the life skills to be absolutely successful in all your endeavours and to succeed intuitively you must know this. When you can acknowledge that your intuition is inherent in you and then apply your soul force to your business, your life, your projects with your existing life skills you will increase your success beyond your current dreams — because you are uniquely creative.

I once sat in a corporate training session and by way of introduction the trainer gave each of us a blank sheet of paper. Each sheet was exactly the same. She asked us to close our eyes while holding the paper in our left hands. Next we were instructed to fold the paper in half. Tear a piece from the top left-hand corner. Fold it again and this time tear a piece from the bottom right corner, and so the instructions went on. After several folds and tears, we opened our eyes, unfolded the paper sheets and compared the patterns with each other. Now, in the group there were twelve executives of different backgrounds and to our surprise we saw that each sheet of paper was a different pattern. This she explained was interesting as her instructions to us were identical yet our interpretations were all different.

Interesting indeed! We all observe reality through our own filters and our own experiences. The patterns that we created on our sheets of paper were unique to each one of us. If her instructions were the only influence affecting our expression then we could hypothesise that all patterns would be the same. So what was the difference in the ingredients? Because the patterns on the sheets of paper were an outward expression of our own creativity, somewhere inside us we had each tapped into our unique creative source, or so it appeared. Remember that the ego can listen to the thoughts of the linear reality or of the soul. In this case, because we had no frame of reference, our egos tapped directly into our soul expression. This exercise is a simple one and is fun to try in a group. Yet besides the interest that it generates, it is a perfect demonstration that you are the difference in your life that makes you unique.

Your ideas and your dreaming start from somewhere. Have you ever wondered where? How you interact with others, whether it be in listening and interpreting another's signals or someone interpreting your expression through their filters, the result is the same. It is unique, one of a kind and therefore unable to be copied. So why do people try to be like someone else, why do they model themselves on another's success no matter how magnificent that success is? Your only potential is within you. It expresses itself in you in many ways. I can't teach you to be like me. My achievements are my achievements and your achievements are your achievements. So in essence neither I nor anyone else can teach you anything at all! Wow! You may be wondering why you bought this book when it can't teach you anything. Please let me explain.

LUCK VS SOULFUL CREATIVITY

Your soul is your best teacher. The environment you live in is your classroom and all your life's experiences are your cur-

riculum. Have you ever wondered why you have done cert
things as you are doing them and only after the event ha
realised why? Have you noticed that often when something
good happens people will say to you, and perhaps you may
even think it yourself, that you have been lucky? How often
have you been in the right place at the right time and achieved
something out of the ordinary and the comment of *Wow! You
were really lucky!* has been levelled at you. Well, let me throw
you a thought. Anyone, even yourself, who implies that your
success is lucky is denying your soul's creative expression and
its ability to create success.

Think about it. Luck by definition is something that is out of
your control and just happens. So why would you want to
believe that your success was a chance happening and that you
were out of control when you succeeded or that you were
lucky? Remember, every time you tell yourself that you were
lucky or accept the notion from another person you are denying your soul's ability to express itself.

The concept of luck is helpful because it explains good
fortune that has no apparent intellectual explanation. Scientifically, we associate luck with the statistically safe calculations of
chance, probability and randomness. When a pattern emerges
that is said to be significant, it is not deemed to be random
chance because it happens more frequently than is deemed
possible randomly. Significant events are then considered to
be reliable and something that you can base your trust on. In
the beginning your soul's expression may appear as a random
event. It will appear to you as something extraordinary or mir-
aculous and possibly explained as a matter of luck. The notion
of miracles is a part of the linear universe. It is an attempt to
explain an event or an occurrence that humankind cannot
explain from its linear experiences.

Your intuitions are significant events. Anything is possible
and is in the realm of your soul's creativity. All events in your
life are a part of your experience. Therefore luck and miracles
have no place in the intuitive realm.

The best method I know to test and prove the validity of the
intuitive process is to record your intuitive thoughts. Buy a
diary and when you get an intuitive flash about anything at all,
note it and wait for it to happen. I promise you that it will. Then
when you witness the reality of your intuition you have a

choice, either you can affirm that it was surely a coincidence or you can acknowledge your intuitive power. This recording process is useful for many reasons. In the next three chapters we will be discovering the difference between ego as an expression of soul, and ego in survival mode. When a thought is intuitive it is absolutely accurate. When fear encases the thought, the ego reacts and moves into the random chance theory. By recording each thought and noting the result of it you will soon learn the difference between these thought processes.

The intuitive approach may be completely untouched ground for you. Alternatively, it may provide an opportunity to sharpen skills that you suspect you have but have not had the courage to tell anyone about. For some, this inner journey to reach their intuitive nature can be equivalent to our first step on the moon. It is my sincere wish that as we walk together on this intuitive moon walk your reserves of excitement and enthusiasm are inexhaustible as you continually discover more about the limitless power that is you.

SUMMARY

1   Intuition is the innate ability that enables us to access the knowledge that is *in*side of ourselves. This library of knowledge contains all the *tuition* we need to grow and expand.

2   Experience and knowledge together are the basis on which to learn how to live intuitively.

3   The teaching process has two components — intellectual and experiential.

4   Learning requires thought *and* action.

5   The ego is the driving force of your personality in the world.

6   We instruct the ego through our thoughts from information drawn either from the linear reality of cause and effect or the multi-dimensional reality of unlimited opportunity.

7   You are your best teacher. The environment you live in is your classroom. Your experience in all of life is your curriculum.

8 We are the basis of human society, and are the footing of organisations and structures that are established to promote group ideas that strive to achieve the common goals of the individual member.

9 When we look at history, humans always seem to be given one fundamental choice. Do we run our lives on the premise of the war of humankind or do we have the courage to travel into our own inner space and learn how to use our intuitive power?

10 You have the life skills to be absolutely successful in all your endeavours and for success on the intuitive levels you must know this. Why? Because you are uniquely creative.

11 Anyone, including yourself, who implies that your success is lucky is denying your own innate power and your intuition to create success.

12 When a thought is intuitive it is absolutely accurate. When a thought is a linear-driven ego response it slips into the random chance theory.

2

A Time to Release the Past

I walked through the country and on to the sea
I did not see the people and they did not see me
I knew I was real and believed them to be
We could not communicate yet we seemed oh so free

I went to the mountains and then to the plains
The animals were absent yet the birds seemed free
I looked at the landscape and felt ever in awe
Why? I wondered, when there was nothing to see

So back to the cities to find out why
About what is illusion and who am I
To observe all humanity in search of the reason
And hopefully return with the answer of the seasons

Now there is talk these days of power and success
And with it I notice the conflict and mess
So where is the peace and the prosperity predicted
Maybe I will find it somewhere unexpected

So I will search for the road that can take me there
In faith and knowing that it is out there, somewhere
And when I find this road that will make me free
I will walk it with just my intuition and me

THE SEASONS AND PHILOSOPHY

Experiencing the earth's seasons is inspirational and their influence has motivated many a romantic to wax lyrically. The seasons influence our moods, our music, the clothes we wear, the houses we build, the type of holiday we take and generally determine many aspects of our lifestyle. The seasons are a part of us and we are a part of the seasons. The seasons are expressive, tactile, feeling, and possess many qualities inherent in our intuition. It is because of the perfect simplicity of this model, that I use it to devise practical applications to achieve project goals, intuitively.

Living Intuitively treats the process of discovering our intuition as a project, like any other, with the aims of understanding it, learning to communicate with it and producing significant results by using it. Once mastered, you can apply the principles of seasonal model to any project, business or life pursuit. They are powerful tools in achieving success across many aspects of our lives.

When we embark upon a project, it is important to recognise the progressive stages inherent in its lifecycle. Then we can focus our efforts directly to the nature of the actual stage that the project is in. The project's success depends on how we apply ourselves to these characteristics, how well we understand each process and how aligned we are to each of the specific energies effecting it.

Over time, I have noticed that these project stages resemble the cyclical progression of the earth's seasons. Ancient cultures observed the natural environment to draw on seasonal characteristics and peculiarities so that they could develop laws of survival and development. The ancient Chinese, in particular, reflected this way of thought. An example is Lao Tse's Taoist philosophy. Indeed most cultures that were close to nature, and relied on the elements for survival, developed sophisticated systems based on their observations of the seasonal cycles of the planet. Sophisticated philosophies emerged as the result of patient observations of the earth's forces and the natural laws. These philosophies proved themselves when put into action. Their pragmatic applications achieved tangible results.

If there must be a start to the seasonal cycle then I believe that it begins at the time of winter. During winter, outward growth stops or at least slows to a minimum. People who live from the produce of the land focus inward to rest, regenerate, fix their tools and plan for the outwardly productive seasons to come.

WINTER DEFINED

Winter is the season of inner cleansing, mental strength, patience and preparation without a lot of external activity. For some, it can be a time when the self confronts the self in the silence of inactivity or perhaps even solitude. For others it can be a time of communicating with loved ones and generally catching up on chores or interests that time did not allow during the more active seasons. Before growth is evidenced in the external world, inner growth starts during winter.

To allow your intuitive skills to develop, the initial emphasis must be on this inner activity while the ongoing emphasis is on developing your inner power to produce intuitive results. The seasonal model can, at first glance, appear linear and you should be wary of becoming trapped in the consciousness of linear time. As our intuitive intelligence develops, so too will our understanding of multi-dimensional time, until we learn to live totally in the present. It is then that neither the past nor the future has relevance.

Similarly, as life is continuous, there is no one reading this book who is at the start of the intuitive growth process. Yet I ask that you accept this illusion for a short time so that you can find your current position in the cycle. When evaluating a project that is currently in progress or when beginning one, it can help to use the illusion of linear time to identify where you are. You can then make the necessary adjustments to align your purpose to the circumstances around you. For example, are you looking for the results of a project before you have planted the seed? Are you ready to harvest results yet still believe you are in the planting season? Order is an integral part of the universe and timing is always important. To go on to a future step without consolidating the present situation can result in achieving less than perfect potential.

Irrespective of our goals, we must always know where we are now, who we are at this present moment and accept it.

That's right. I said accept it! Accept who you are now, accept the situation you are in, and love it because it is the basis of your growth. Your present situation will teach you about yourself, will provide you with the experiences to show you your talents and will motivate you to help release unconscious thought patterns that will inhibit your growth.

We talk of linear time. We hear of past events, belief systems and hurts that accommodate the illusion of stagnation. Some will talk of past-life associations and the need to release karma. Notice they will say old-karma. Yet whatever it is that is affecting our lives now, is real NOW. It is, if you like, NOW karma! The past is an illusion that can, should we choose to allow it, retard our progress and stop our intuitive development. Our intuition lives now. It is a now phenomenon and exists in all dimensions simultaneously.

Your intuition is a part of you. It is yours and belongs to you. To develop intuitively, you will develop greater levels of trust in yourself the more that you work with it. You will find its benefits in pragmatic living. It will relate to your lifestyle, how you perceive and relate to others, and how you develop leadership qualities. By developing your intuitive side your life will significantly prosper, flourish and grow — as will the lives of those with whom you interact. In other words, it is by our experiences that the soul learns, heals itself and grows. It is these experiences that provide the springboard for our learning and subsequent life's growth. Therefore, all of life's experiences are one hundred per cent relevant to our development.

We do not have to simulate artificial situations to release negative beliefs and emotional states. By living in the 'now' every situation and circumstance is here for us. Should we avoid living in our experiences then we are denying the opportunity to prosper now. Everything is right for us now. Everything is right in yesterday's now just as it is in tomorrow's now.

It is by allowing our intuition to arrive into consciousness, being able to recognise it, being able to use it and being able to create with it that identifies us as intuitive people. Intuition, by nature, is absolutely effective now and it is innate in us. The skills taught in this book relate to finding it, communicating with it and applying it.

Winter is a time to release the past. It is the time to clear out any factors in our lives that are no longer relevant to make room for the new. You may well ask how do we release the past?

The answer simply put is by affirming the present. Practise thinking in the NOW because there is no reality left in the past. If it is still with us then our past is our present and it is in the present that we all live, either consciously or unconsciously.

AN EXAMPLE

Let's reflect on the model of the farmer who works every day to produce crops in some future now. Along the way he buys machinery and maybe before that he builds a huge barn. This building stores all his equipment and the harvest. It is his work-shop and his creative centre. Over time the equipment he bought deteriorates through constant use. His experiences are useful and productive. He comes to depend on them. He looks upon them with affection, relies on them and loves them. So when they are no longer of use to him, he keeps the memories and stores them in an unused part of the barn. Now the machinery sits there. It provides a home for mice. Birds build their nests in it and it collects dust. Yet the machinery still serves a purpose because it encourages him through the hard times. If nothing else, when he looks at it, his spirits rise.

Over time, more and more memorabilia, that once had creative value, finds a way into the corner of the barn. Until one day the farmer realises that these memories have taken all the space in his creative centre. He now has nowhere to place his workbench, garage his new equipment or store his harvest. He feels that the past has caught up with him. In reality, his past never left him! He keeps it in the present, and this cluttered life restricts his ability to create new crops and causes frustration, anxiety and perhaps even depression. His neighbours ask him what has happened to his farm and why is he depressed? They talk among themselves that 'he is not the man he used to be'. The farmer, on the other hand, complains that he cannot get on top of things. If only he had the money to build a new barn. If only he had time to start new projects. All he seems to do is fix old equipment and so on.

At this moment, the farmer has become a 'victim'. Not to outside influences, but rather to his reluctance to recognise that the tools that were so useful to him and that served him well need releasing. He has become a victim to himself.

LETTING GO

Often we are reluctant to let go of patterns, memories and relationships that served us perfectly yet are no longer relevant to our lifestyles. We would feel guilty to let them go. We even feel insecure at the thought of releasing them, so we keep them in the present. It is not our past that is holding us back. It is our refusal to let go of outmoded 'things' in our lives and because of this it is our 'present' that is retarding our progress and we stagnate. Water becomes foul when it stands still for too long and so does our intuition. Our intuition is dynamic, moving, searching. It is passionate. It is alive and exciting.

Our intuition is a vibrant energy that can't live fully in stagnation. It needs room to grow and flourish. It needs energy to strengthen its muscles. It needs movement to be flexible now. When we release the past by affirming the present, we in effect acknowledge consciously that everything that is in and is a part of our lives is real and tangible now. Once we recognise this and affirm our complete power of choice, we strengthen our abilities to confront these 'accoutrements'. By exploring our inner warehouses and exercising our powers of choice, we experience the freedom that is necessary for our intuition to surface. The development of your intuition will be distinctive because your experiences are different. You must recognise this. Your intuition will manifest uniquely. It is uniquely yours.

WAIT FOR THE RESULTS

The best way to develop intuitively is slowly, day by day. There is no instant packet mix to speed up the process. I remember when I started to develop intuitively I held a lot of irrational fear about the process. At the same time I was impatient to develop quickly. My teacher was recommended to me because of her pragmatism, common sense and ability to tell it how it is. In other words, when I went off in the clouds, Jan would firmly plant my feet back on earth — sometimes up to my neck! Very early in our teacher/student relationship Jan looked me straight in the eye and told me that the process would take about six years to do it properly. I nodded in agreement. Then, secretly, I thought that I would surprise her by doing it faster.

This impatience to develop often caused me pain and frustration. On one occasion when Rassoon, Jan's guide, appeared in the class, I asked him how I could speed up my development. Rassoon replied: 'My friend, in your rush to the well, you tripped over the bucket and spilt the water that you had collected in it'. This was my first encounter with a spirit guide manifesting through a psychic in trance. I thought Jan's guide was a fruitcake! Reflecting back, I now realise he was very wise. I pass the same advice on to you. Be patient as you grow.

The universe is a logically ordered place and there are specific cycles we must experience, understand and learn from so that we can develop. My impatience led me to ignore the winter time of my development, which meant that I had to work harder at it. I did learn, however, a magnificent lesson about patience. The seasons wait for no one. The choice that we have is how we experience them. I sometimes feel that the winter is the most difficult season because there appears little to do, lots of darkness, and growth seems to be so slow. Yet as we embark upon the winter time of our intuitive development we need to recognise what is around us. We must delve into our inner storehouses and recognise what is there so that we can understand who we are now. In this way we can use the time effectively in preparing, planning and clearing the ground for our intuitive growth. So be patient and expect results.

Our intuition manifests from within. We then change with it, sometimes in subtle ways. So subtle at times that we overlook the changes as they happen. We will discuss this further in the chapters on spring to summer. In your diary, record your dreams, record your feelings and relate them to everyday events.

In the cold climates winter is a time to stay indoors. It provides the opportunity for people to reflect on their experiences and to review their philosophies of life. With the growth of your intuitive self, your beliefs and philosophies change. People around you will also notice this change and respond to you differently. Understand that they too are changing and be flexible in your attitude towards them. With the emergence of your intuitive self, you will find evidence of your spiritual self.

Spiritual growth occurs when healing takes place over the many planes of our being. Each spark of the divine, which makes up the soul of the universe, drives each one of us to further understand ourselves and hence increase our understanding of soul. This is the quest that we are all on whether we consciously recognise it or not and succeed we must, according to our experiences, understanding and will. By taking personal responsibility for our experiences we change, grow and develop our intuitive power.

WORKSHOP *(allow one hour)*

Most chapters of *Living Intuitively* contain two distinct sections. The first section is to do with explanations about intuition. This is the intellectual part of the teaching. Remember the example of reader response in Chapter One. The second section headed 'WORKSHOP' is the doing part of the book. Both are important. You will find that, as your understanding of intuition grows, you will be able to add to the theory sections from your own experiences. And the workshops will be a catalyst for the ongoing development of your intuitive ability.

You may benefit initially by asking a friend to read the instructions to you. Always remember to bring your work book/diary to these sessions and allow time to write your thoughts and experiences at the end of each sitting. Now, find a quiet, comfortable place where you will remain undisturbed for one hour.

EXERCISE ONE *(allow fifteen minutes)*

Please consider the following statement:

At this time in your life, everything is right in your world and your prosperity is assured

Now you may believe this to be a wild and irrational statement. After all, look at all the events and happenings in your life that are completely out of your control. The people around you don't listen to you and they don't give you what you want. You are so full of social conditioning that you sometimes act like an android and wonder if you really have a say at all.

Please consider the statement again.

At this time in your life, everything is right in your world and your prosperity is assured

Relax some more, assume a comfortable position and take three deep breaths. Breathe as deeply as you can and then on the exhale let go of all your tension.

Now say it with me.

At this time in my life, everything is right in my world and my prosperity is assured

Let's say it again.

At this time in my life, everything is right in my world and my prosperity is assured

Say it again, aloud with real conviction, feeling this statement in every cell of your body.

At this time in my life, everything is right in my world and my prosperity is assured

While you were repeating this statement to yourself did you notice the thoughts that seemed to come from nowhere? It doesn't matter exactly what they were. The interesting thing is, that as you made this statement, something happened. As yet we don't know what. This statement did, however, stimulate at least one thought. If we were to consult a neurologist, and ask for a measurement of that thought, chances are she/he would describe it as a brainwave or an electrical charge or impulse. Now we know and recognise electricity as energy so we could say that this statement created energy. To continue further, we also know that if we use energy in certain ways, it can create specific happenings, phenomena and events.

Go back to the statement.

At this time in my life, everything is right in my world and my prosperity is assured

What thoughts and emotions did it produce? Write them down now because they will reveal hidden thought patterns that are affecting your development. Did you feel empowered? Did you believe that everything *is* right in your world. Maybe it brought up other feelings and thoughts that were far from empowering? The point is that our very thoughts determine who we are, what we are about, and all facets of the situations in which we find ourselves. Ah-ha, you say. This is all about positive thinking. In a way it is. It's a lot more than that too.

Consider that from birth and maybe even before, the intelligent part of us was experiencing our environment, thinking about the experiences, observing which actions caused what effect and formulating beliefs or rules that would, from then on, run our lives. Can you see how our thoughts have contributed significantly to whom we are now?

As we grew up we observed those with whom we interacted. We listened to their beliefs and adopted some of them as 'road rules of life'. We have gradually formulated and built up a system of beliefs, expectations and interactions. All based on our observations. As children, our filters were open, less critical and more accepting than as adults. Therefore it was possible that we accepted half-truths, misunderstandings and experiences that we took out of context to form the foundation of our personal laws of survival, success and happiness.

Should some of your beliefs tend toward the negative, I would expect that you are suffering problems in health, relationships, financial affairs, or just general areas of dissatisfaction with your life. It is not for me or anyone else to judge what is right or wrong with your life, nor is your own critical judgement about your life beneficial. Set aside right now all self-criticism and view the past with feelings of gratitude. It is these experiences that create the wisdom to support you now and provide the springboard for your intuitive development.

It is possible to create energy through statements. It is also possible that our thoughts create chemical reactions in our bodies that affect our health, vitality and intellectual processes, because our statements and thoughts do affect the very essence of our existence. Then it is important that we take particular care to create within ourselves the best possible thoughts, beliefs and attitudes. This will empower us to receive all the prosperity that is waiting to pour into our lives.

During the winter time of our development it is necessary to look into our personal storehouses and recognise just what thoughts, beliefs and attitudes live there. When we discover any unwanted thoughts, then we need to learn how to release them. In *Living Intuitively* we practise how to lovingly disallow further negative beliefs from entering our existence. We will use the three powerful tools of forgiveness, release and denial. Before we get to that, let's take a few minutes to relax and work on that positive statement introduced earlier. Can you remember what it is?

The statement is:

At this time in my life, everything is right in my world and my prosperity is assured

Whenever you feel that life is not treating you fairly. Relax and feel the power in this statement.

EXERCISE TWO *(allow thirty minutes)*

The following is a guided meditation that will assist you to get in touch with your intuitive being.

Remain in a comfortable position and take several deep breaths, relaxing further as you release each breath. As you inhale, either say aloud or in your thoughts 'I AM that I AM' and as you exhale allow all of yourself to relax more deeply than before.

Now breathe in deeply saying to yourself:

I AM that I AM

Continue to exhale and relax more deeply than before. Breathe in deeply and say:

I AM that I AM

Exhale and relax more deeply than before. Breathe in deeply and say:

I AM that I AM

Exhale and relax more deeply than before. Breathe in deeply and say:

I AM that I AM

Exhale and relax more deeply than before.

Now see yourself sitting beside the most beautiful mountain rock pool that you have ever experienced. The sun's rays are streaming down creating perfect warmth and a feeling of complete harmony and peace. Nothing can harm you here. You are totally safe and protected. Your awareness drifts to the gentle sound of water falling at the side of the pool. You notice that the sun's rays are dancing off the spray and turning the light into the colours of the rainbow. These lights dance effortlessly on the gentle breeze. See the colours, feel the colours, feel the peace, enjoy this place.

It is now time to meditate for about fifteen minutes concentrating on the only statement that has meaning and purpose in your world at this time.

At this time in my life, everything is right in my world and my prosperity is assured

After you have completed the meditation, remember that this quiet, most glorious place is now a part of you, where you can go at any time you choose.

When you finish each meditation, visualise a white mist descending over you and covering you from head to foot. Tell yourself that you feel lighter and energised, knowing that perfect healing and perfect intuitive growth are taking place in your life now and most certainly:

At this time in my life, everything is right in my world and my prosperity is assured

Take all the time you need to absorb what happened and use your journal to record any thoughts and inspirations that you want to keep for your future lessons or reflections. The recording of the information that surfaced from your meditation is the framework of your intuitive growth.

SUMMARY

1   The seasons influence our moods, our music, the clothes we wear, the houses we build, the type of holiday we take and generally control significant aspects of our lifestyle.

2   The principles of seasonal model can be applied to any project, business or life pursuit and are powerful tools in achieving success across many aspects of our lives.

3   The season cycle begins in winter. Winter time is the season for inner cleansing, mental strength, patience and preparation without a lot of external activity. It is the time when the self confronts the self in silence.

4   To allow our intuitional skills to develop, the initial emphasis is on inner activity.

5   Whatever our goals, we must first identify where we are now, who we are at this present moment and accept it.

6   Whatever is affecting our lives now is real NOW. Our memories have an effect on the present. The past is an

illusion that can, should we choose to allow it, retard our progress and stop our intuitive development.

7   We have no need to simulate artificial situations to release the negative beliefs and emotional states that are slowing our development. By living in the 'now' every situation and circumstance is there for us.

8   Winter is the time to release the past. It is the time to clear out any factors in our lives that have no more relevance so that we can make room for the new.

9   As our intuition manifests from within, we change with it, sometimes in subtle ways. So subtle at times that we overlook changes when they happen.

10   Spiritual growth occurs when healing takes place over the many planes of our being.

11   Taking personal responsibility totally for our experiences is the most important way to effect positive change, growth and to develop our intuitive power.

3

*First Clear
the Water*

*The first fall of snow, the snap chill in the air, the pleasure
of the new. Animals disappear to the safety of the earth.
During winter, Mother Earth protects and nurtures all life
seeking refuge in her.*

*It is a fool that wanders the snow without clothes, and it is
the sage who recognises the advantages of this time.*

*Fire is important. It heats, it cleanses, it purifies and it
supports life. So collect your wood and keep it dry. Make
sure your house is free of draughts and secure against the
elements.*

*Winter is a time to batten down, to stay put, and to work
with the soul. In the silence, be still, speak with your heart
and choose to clear out all that is no longer furthering your
life's growth.*

Y OU MAY BE wondering why each chapter starts with a poem
or piece of metaphorical prose. Since working with people
dedicated to their intuitive development, I have observed several characteristic patterns.

First, when we block our intuition, it helps to talk to it in
abstract terms. Intuition is very much like water and can seep in
and around solid objects with ease. Like water, it will gradually
soften the blocks and break them down into small particles so
that the stream can take them away. Intuition often comes out
of left field. By this I mean that it comes in a way that we don't
expect. Do you see where expectations can hinder the emergence of an intuitive thought into consciousness?

Second, the use of symbolism helps to break down intellectual rigidity to free intuitive expression.

Third, intuition is about emotional flow and rhythm. It is
about creative flow. Poetry and metaphor both can touch our
own poetic sensibilities and encourage our intuition to express
itself.

Now that we have fed our intellect with rational explanations let's begin to use our imagination to bring out our
intuitive skills.

INTUITION AND THE HIGH DIVER

Imagine that you want to be a world-champion high diver. You
have never dived competitively before yet you have an ever-
increasing urge within you — some may call it intuitive — to do
it. What's interesting, you observe, is the ever present knowledge within you, that you *will* win the World Championship. In
fact, these feelings are so strong that you decide to begin the
project to become the world's number one diver. This imaginary example is powerfully symbolic. The water symbolises our
intuition. Our project is to dive perfectly into it.

Let's take our first walk up the ladder, to about twenty
metres, and stand rather cautiously at the back of the platform.
Wow! From up here we see the risk that any strong cross-wind
can blow us off if we are not careful. Take a mental note that it's
unsafe to be on the platform when there are strong gusts about.
To make the world-championship dive we need a calm day.
Fortunately today is such a day. So let's move closer to the
platform's edge and look down. From this height the pool
looks so small that it is difficult to see any water in it.

When we first start to practise living intuitively, it can feel a lot like standing on the diving platform. Our intuition seems so tiny and insignificant compared to the rest of our surroundings. Because we haven't come up close to it and we don't know it intimately, it seems to us that it is 'out there' somewhere. These reactions are common at this stage; so just accept them without placing too much importance on them. We are so tentative, we tend to shuffle towards our intuition. I've noticed that people I train tend to solicit the support of their friends when they are unsure of their intuition. Their friends' opinions are important to them, especially when they are reassuring. Of course, your friends may hold strong opinions — this is absolutely normal — but strong opinions can have the same effect as strong gusts of wind when you are on the diving tower. Make sure that the opinions of others don't blow you off your perch. If they take you unawares then certainly they will.

Living intuitively is an inner process. Our intellectual belief systems of externalisation suggest that everything we need is out there somewhere. Intuition is within us because it is a part of us. Indeed, it is us! Therefore it is personal. No one else can fully understand what your intuition means to you, just as you can't fully appreciate another's intuitive expression. To this extent living intuitively can feel, at times, just like you are the lone high diver.

Pause for a moment and visualise standing on the platform and note any feelings as they emerge. We have seen divers perform at this height with ease, yet knowing that someone else has dived successfully is not reassuring. If fear and doubt are present, it is because we have never done this before. There is no precedent in our lives to suggest that we can perform a dive such as this and survive. Sure we've jumped off the one-metre board, maybe even the three-metre board, but twenty metres, never! The task seems too daunting; yet the sense that we are the world-champion diver is still as strong as before.

Standing at the platform's edge, a chill of uncertainty is present around us. We know that the winter time of our project has begun. Being up here on the platform generates many diverse thoughts, feelings, and emotions. Standing here in contemplation you notice a warm presence around you. Take your awareness to your hands. Hold them relaxed and quite still. Observe the warmth or tingling sensation of comfort coming into them. This sensation spreads from your palms to the backs of your hands and flows through your body until you feel enfolded in warmth and safety. It feels like there is a presence around you. It is warm, calming and has a sense of absolute wisdom about it. This presence, this wisdom is something we feel that we can trust. We listen to it and it suggests that we come down from the tower. It is not time for the dive. First we need to become familiar with the pool close up. That way we will be more at ease when it is time to make the first practice dive.

This is the time for preparation. Before making the dive we must satisfy ourselves that:

1   There is sufficient water in the pool. (Your intuition is there.)
2   The pool is deep enough. (Your intuition can support you.)
3   There is nothing in the water to injure us. (Your ego won't get in the way.)
4   The water is clean enough to dive into. (Your intentions are soul-directed.)

On our way down the ladder we think back to the story about the farmer with the cluttered barn. Questions rise up from within us. We wonder about whether we are inwardly prepared to make the first practice dive? What if the water level is too low? What if there are objects floating in the pool? Maybe our first step should be to clear the water. Self-doubts are the very things that will bring us to grief when we try to live intuitively. The old saying: 'if in doubt — don't' applies here. It's one thing to practise. It is another to apply it to real-life situations. People who live intuitively are people who are confident in the knowledge that their intuition is infallible. They have played with it and tested its validity until they are one hundred per cent confident in it. This is the purpose of these practice sessions; to get to know yourself without the restriction of beliefs that bring back the very past that you would like to be rid of. Address self-doubts as soon as they become evident because once they are dealt with they transform into a positive understanding of who you are.

THE INTUITIVE POOL

Consider that the pool represents your intuitive well and the water your intuition. By clearing the pool we are looking at our ego blocks, present conditioning and any belief that could prevent the perfect entry of the dive. Previously we touched on the notion that our thoughts create our reality, and our environment is a projection of these thoughts. Similarly, we use thought to bring our intuition into consciousness.

Intuition links us to the source of all energy, wisdom and universal love. It acts as the water hose, if you like, between the infinite universal pool of knowledge and our creativity. As we draw from the universal source and our intuitive wells begin to fill, there is an automatic cleansing of the water. Once our blocks surface we have the choice to remove them from our lives or leave them where they are.

If this hose has been unused for a while it may well have lost its flexibility. Your intuition, however, will regulate the flow to maintain a comfortable pressure. Considering this, each person's intuitive development is different because it depends on the flexibility and strength of the hose to allow the intuitive stream to flow through it. Do you remember in the previous chapter when I mentioned spilling my bucket in the rush to the well? Appropriately, this is where patience and trust are imperative. Your intuition accesses total and complete wisdom. It comes from a point of absolute integrity and will ensure your complete safety.

A GLIMPSE OF THE EGO

Should you become impatient and try to run before you can walk your ego will take over and your intuition will recede. Remember that it is always our choice whether we wish to function from the perspective of ego, or function in co-operation and harmony with the soul. The flotsam and jetsam in our intuitive well is the creation of our ego. It is irrelevant whether the obstacle originates from another person or not. The fact remains that it is there in our intuitive pool because we created it and allowed it in. There is absolutely no need to feel guilty about this. We are completely responsible for our lives and the good news is that because we created the blocks, or let them in, we have the absolute power to lovingly remove them.

In this context, I am referring to the ego in the linear sense. I'm talking about the part of us that seeks to detach from the concept of universal oneness or wholeness. It is the part of us that believes in the limitation of resources and hence tries to acquire prosperity by taking from others and using another's resources for its own benefit. From this perspective, ego accepts and creates limitation. It steeps itself in negativity, judgement and criticism while continually seeking praise and recognition from others. Over the years, and by observing my ego, I have developed a simple rule. When I act from the linear perspective of ego, I hurt the people around me and ultimately myself. When I act from the soul perspective of ego, I expand my consciousness, increase my ability to love people close to me and subsequently myself. To live in a linear ego state is to dwell in illusion, negativity, fear and constriction. To be one with my soul means that I become conscious, aware, fearless and infinitely powerful.

INTUITION AND THE NINE DOTS

This is a game commonly played in training courses. It's where the saying 'to think outside the nine dots' came from. Connect the nine dots below without taking your pen or pencil off the paper. Use four straight lines to connect all the dots. The lines should be continuous.

Diagram 2 – Lateral thinking exercise (solution on p.175)

A clue to the solution is that you must expand your consciousness and extend the lines outside of the nine dots.

People categorised as restrictive problem-solvers work within the confines of the nine dots. Lateral thinkers are said to work both within and outside the nine dots. And 'cosmic wombats' live outside the nine dots all the time.

The way our intuition works is by moving in and out of the nine dots freely. Consider that the area inside the perimeter of the nine dots represents the linear reality. The products of this world are measured in terms of tangible benefits such as a new car, an overseas holiday, a new house and so on. The products that sit outside the nine dots are qualities, for example, happiness, fulfilment, freedom, sense of life's purpose and so on. These typically cannot be measured in tangible, touchable terms. The tangible products that sit within the nine dots are products created by your ego-driven personality. The area inside the nine dots I define as the linear world or reality. The products that sit outside of the nine dots that the linear perspective cannot measure, are goals of the soul. The area outside of the nine dots I define as the multi-dimensional world or reality. Look at the following diagram.

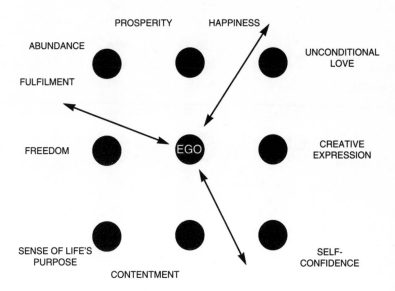

Diagram 3 – The ego moves freely between linear reality and multi-dimensional reality.

Notice the central dot. We sit in the absolute centre of both worlds or realities. The ego can move freely around drawing information from either reality whenever it chooses. Providing the inner zone is block free you will have access to limitless potential. The ego can move outside the linear framework, seek the wisdom of the soul and bring it back into the linear dimension to create perfectly. This is what I mean when I talk about infinite possibility and opportunity. The ego sits at the centre and moves around the realities intuitively. The role of intuition in this model is as the communicator across zones.

Now we discussed earlier that the ego can draw from either reality. If you have a belief system that is restrictive then the model may look like this.

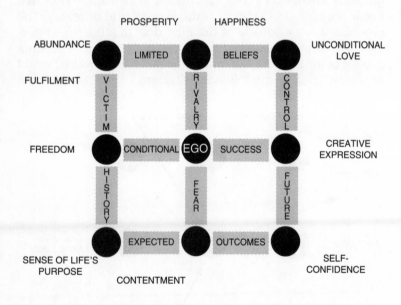

Diagram 4 – Restrictive beliefs create barriers between linear reality and multi-dimensional reality.

Notice how fences have been built within and around the linear world. These fences are the blocks to intuitive communication. Depending on how strong the blocks are and where they are, they can either block the information flow altogether or misdirect the information. This misdirection is the illusion that I talk of in the linear reality. Please note that it doesn't have to be this way. The more blocks that are in place around the ego the more difficult soul communication becomes until we lose sight of the total picture. Once we become blinkered, our intuition can't work effectively because it will miss the mark so-to-speak. The confusion that results looks something like this:

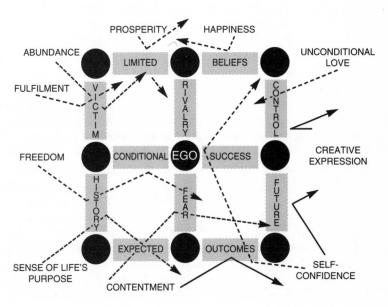

Diagram 5 – Intuition is interrupted and misdirected by ego blocks.

Addressing our blocks and clearing them out is vital to our intuitive expression.

IDENTIFYING THE BLOCKS

How do we identify these obstacles floating in our intuitive pools? The emergence of intuitive thought rises from deep within us. It manifests as conscious thought. If our ego cannot distinguish between belief patterns and soul desires then intuitive hunches will remain just that. Sometimes they will prove accurate and sometimes not. Remember that thoughts generated from illusion will manifest short of our ultimate good. So, when our plans and goals spring from our belief systems, we only have the illusion of progressing towards these goals. In reality, we are producing results to justify and reinforce the belief systems. In this situation the successes we aim for will never happen.

This is why projects fail and fade away before fully realising their goals. For each of us to achieve our life's goals, it is imperative to recognise the difference between belief patterns and soul-generated thought. In other words, the first step towards utilising your intuition is to know yourself and be prepared to view the world honestly. All of which is of your creation.

Our environment is simply a projection of ourself. To view life in this context is similar to watching a film. The difference is that life's images are sourced from our spiritual personalities rather than from celluloid. Clues to help us understand our spiritual status are embedded in our daily lives. By identifying events in our environment that we perceive as external problems, we can see our games, understand them and lovingly let them go. When our blocks and inhibitors surface, it is good news. Why? Because these problems only become visible when the soul knows that we are ready, willing and able to transform them. I'll give you an example.

A client had an idea about a new type of business that he knew would work. He told me that it felt like his life's purpose and that he thought he knew how to achieve it. A prerequisite, or so he thought, was to obtain funding by the way of capital loans. So off he went to sell the idea. Those whom he approached received him well. Their reactions confirmed that the concept was exciting, ambitious and that he was breaking new ground. However, no one wanted to invest the total amount required.

He approached me in a state of frustration, with his anger focusing on the potential investors who only wanted to commit seventy-five per cent to his proposal — the remaining twenty-five per cent was unfunded. He created the belief that total funding was essential before he could take the next step, and the more he became entrenched in this attitude the more his creativity dried up.

After we looked at his belief systems he realised that the obstacles placed in his path by the lenders were merely a reflection of his beliefs about himself. First, he received only seventy-five per cent commitment because he recognised within himself the reluctance to ever complete a project one hundred per cent. Why? Because of his impatience.

Second, he viewed any criticism as a slur on his ability. These people did not have one hundred per cent confidence in him. Why? Because he did not have one hundred per cent confidence in himself. Like everything in life, he realised that he had a choice to make. He could accept the situation, give up and reinforce the belief (the illusion) that he could only have seventy-five per cent of something, or he could choose to change. So change he did.

He looked into his intuitive well from the perspective of the soul and recognised that he judged these people as negative influences. He mapped out a four-point plan to effect the change.

Step 1:

He changed his attitude by viewing every criticism as positive. Those critics were not there to impede his success. They were there to teach him how to be successful. Instead of criticising them, he began to praise and thank them. He listened to what they had to say and made the necessary adjustments.

Step 2:

He recognised his impatience and saw it for the first time as showing in the project as lack of detail. He went back to the drawing board until he got it right. In other words he changed his seventy-five per cent belief system to one hundred per cent success.

Step 3:

He affirmed one hundred per cent confidence in the quality of the information he would present and his ability to do so.

Step 4:

He stopped doubting his ability and affirmed his absolute effectiveness without questioning it.

When you start to clear your intuitive pool, it is important to identify the present situation according to your belief systems, personality and the reactions of others towards you. I have found that when people react unreasonably towards me, there is an aspect of their behaviour that represents that part of me that is creating the block. By clearing out old beliefs, we release the thoughts that are the part of our lives that create the very situations we want to resolve. Clearing out is a process of eliminating and releasing from our consciousness. It is quite simple. All it requires is an attitude of love, discipline and commitment on our part.

When we identify the beliefs that clutter our pools, we can get rid of them conclusively by affirming their positive attributes. This act of affirmation converts them into strengths and eliminates any negative influence that they may have on us. Notice that by eliminating them we are not throwing them out. We transform the negatives into positives. By changing the face of the problem, we release it.

Think back to the farmer who cluttered his barn with unwanted memorabilia. Memorabilia that had remained in his warehouse because of his attachment to it. Now he has choices to make. He can push all the unwanted bits outside the barn and leave them lying around. He can build other barns to house his memorabilia and use all his resources in non-productive effort to maintain these attachments. Alternatively he can recognise their past usefulness and free himself from the belief that they are useful now.

He may also recognise that they have a positive use for some other purpose and give them away. In other words, by recycling what has lost its usefulness to him, he can eliminate his negative blocks. By offering his outdated machinery to the world, someone will pick it up and benefit from it. It's a win-win situation.

The same process will assist you in clearing your pool. First, convert what you can to the positive and, second, release those outmoded aspects and memories. There is nothing in your mind that is inherently bad or evil; the linear state of the ego creates the illusion of good and evil.

Back to the high-diving project. We are about to embark on something that we have not, as yet, experienced. Our feeling of safety rests on the understanding of our experiences. We will need to let go some of our experiences in order to develop our intuition. It takes courage to do this. As we create new supportive experiences we build a new platform. Courage is often required less when understanding increases. Again, should you feel deficient in courage when releasing current conditioning, remember that the universe is an infinite source of courage which you can draw on through your intuition. In meditation you can intuitively connect with the soul and ask for the courage to clear the water.

INTUITION AND INTELLECT — THE TWO EYES

Becoming intuitive defies most established laws of logic because we manifest it in our feelings — not through our intellect. The difficulty with feelings is that there is no way to quantify them from an intellectual point of view. We cannot touch them, see them with our eyes or hear them. Yet it is through our feelings that we recognise intuitive thought. You will hear psychics talk about seeing with their sixth sense. Today, the 'snag' (sensitive new age guy) attracts attention because he has recognised the value of being in touch with his feelings. I find it ironic that some ambitious professional business women have adopted the intellectual approach at the expense of their intuition whereas men have always used traditional logic when competing in the corporate arena. In the 'battle of the sexes' such women, in their drive for equality, are losing touch with their intuition.

Intuition is often symbolised by the element of water. The element of air symbolises intellectualism and indeed intellectuals do seem to 'blow hard' at times when expressing a purely intellectual point of view. Intuition is said to be a feminine quality symbolised by the colour blue. Many people use the sound of running water to enhance a meditative state, or walk along a beach, sit beside a river to relax and find inspiration. Look at the contemplative fisher-people who sit for hours without a bite and who tell you that they love it. Surely for them there is more to fishing than catching the fish.

To recognise intuitive thought is to feel it and to let go of intellectual thought processes. It helps to work with the symbology of nature and feel the understanding. To understand intuitive thought, understand the characteristics of water, observe it in all its states from steam to ice, running and stagnant and you will learn. If this is sounding a bit too esoteric for you, please understand that you are entering into a world that I cannot teach you about unless you let go of logic and extend your ability to feel. Intuitive thought is still pragmatic and can be applied in practical ways to your daily life. You need to realise that intuition operates on several dimensions concurrently including the intellectual. Intellectual thought without the intuitive influence is by definition linear and is a part of the illusory world of cause and effect.

I am writing this message on a flat piece of paper. The words that you are reading you see as flat and one-dimensional. Yet you feel that the words and their meanings are multi-dimensional, with body. They are able to generate emotion and thoughts. All of which find form through your experience. We must not underestimate what we take on board from our experiences and how our responses can become conditioned.

So, intuitive growth is about learning to use our feelings as a sensory receptor, just like our eyes, ears, nose and sense of touch. Our feelings are powerful receptors of information. When translated through our thought processes our feelings become a strong and dynamic force.

Think back to the moments when you had your most successful ideas and on what you were doing at the time. Reflect on the times when you had a sudden impulse and acted on it to discover that you were really 'lucky' — whoops I let that one slip didn't I? Our intuitive thoughts often come to us when we least expect them. You may be in the shower or taking an exhilarating walk along a beach or doing something that is relaxing that takes your mind off the troubles of the day. This is the way that intuitive thoughts arrive into our consciousness.

MEDITATION — THE KEY TO THE SOUL

We must be able to distinguish between soul communication (intuition) and ego desire (linear thought). There are many personal growth courses of many persuasions that can teach you how to do this. However, I believe that all you need to do is learn how to meditate, and be honest with yourself. There is nothing more to it than that. We meditate to reach a state of relaxation where we can let go of the tension and stress that blocks our ability to recognise intuitive thought. Meditation is nothing more than a disciplined approach to relaxing your being. Meditation will allow the unconscious thought patterns, which help to determine your reality, to surface into a conscious form. It's no more difficult than that. Many people seem to have great battles in those parts of their lives that they wish to change. When you think that something is difficult and when you put effort into breaking a pattern, you are adding weight and giving credence to the problem and reinforcing its existence.

Life *is* easy. There is total truth and wisdom in everything that is. The life force that is you is completely intelligent. It has your best interests at heart because it is you. Therefore if you wish to change and leave aspects of your life behind you need to recognise what they are then bid them farewell and get on with the positives. Trust that the infinite life force will, in time, balance you and heal you.

All truth, by its very nature, stands naked and unashamed. It is tested over all experiences of life. It requires no embellishment. It is only through our attempts to avoid change that we inhibit our happiness, restrict our sense of fulfilment and fail to actualise our prosperity.

The intuitive person learns how to let go of control in whatever form it takes. To work effectively with your intuition you must know yourself and be committed to your personal growth and prosperity.

WORKSHOP *(allow one hour)*

Allow yourself one hour to do this workshop. Find a comfortable, quiet place free of distractions where you can work with the following exercises.

EXERCISE ONE *(allow fifteen minutes)*

Imagine standing on your diving tower and looking down at the water. The tower is twenty metres high and you are about to launch yourself downwards. You stand right at the platform's edge with your toes dangling into open air. Relax and visualise this moment. Take note of your feelings and thoughts at this time. When you feel you have visualised enough, write down all the feelings and thoughts that came up for you, in your intuitive workbook. These notes will crystallise, over time, into the reasons that are holding you back from reaching your goals.

Begin any project with this visualisation. It will help you to recognise any beliefs that you have about yourself that can bring down the project. This is the start of clearing your pool. You can use this exercise as a way of looking inwards to release your blocks, or you can visualise the pool as the project that you want to launch.

EXERCISE TWO (allow thirty minutes)

Earlier I mentioned that it is important for the intuitive person to learn how to let go. Once you start this process through meditation, it will continue well after the meditation finishes until you intuitively rebalance.

Focus your attention on the lower part of your back, near the base of the spine. Visualise the colour orange flowing into it filling up your body.

Breathe deeply and affirm as you breathe in:

I AM Divine Love

Exhale and relax more deeply than before. Breathe deeply and affirm as you breathe in:

I AM Divine Love

Exhale and relax more deeply than before. Breathe deeply and affirm as you breathe in:

I AM Divine Love

Exhale and relax more deeply than before. Breathe deeply and affirm as you breathe in:

I AM Divine Love

Exhaling and relaxing more deeply than before.

As you relax deeper and deeper you become aware of a river. The sun streams down filling you with warmth and energy. Look around you. Take in the vibrant shades of greens and yellows in the vegetation. Notice a boat with luxuriously soft cushions resting at the riverbank.

Step into the boat and recline on the cushions. The boat starts to move gently into the middle of the river. No harm can reach you. You are safe and at peace.

Stay with this scene in meditation for twenty minutes and go where the boat takes you. Observe any people or events that have caused or are causing you pain as they appear to you from the safety of the riverbank. If you choose, you can forgive them, release them from your life and then disallow them any more effect on you now or in the future.

As you come out of your meditation affirm:

I am divine love and forgiveness. I willingly forgive all and know that I am forgiven, I release all negativity from me to its highest good.
   I deny that any negativity can again affect my life.

As you come back now, know that you can take this journey as often as you require. Visualise a beautiful blue light flowing over you from head to foot as if it were a shower washing you. Take whatever time you need to absorb the meditation and write down any thoughts and inspirations that you want to keep for your future lessons and reflections.

SUMMARY

1   Intuition links us to the source of all energy, wisdom and universal love.

2   We are completely responsible for our lives and this is good news because it means that we have absolute power over any blocks that we have created or accepted and can lovingly remove them from our intuitive pools.

3   The linear reality of the ego is that drive in us that believes in limitation of resources and hence tries to acquire prosperity by taking from others and using another's resources for its own benefit.

4   To live only in the linear reality is to dwell in illusion, negativity, fear and constriction. When we are one with the soul we become conscious, aware, fearless and infinitely powerful.

5   Every aspect of your physical world is a manifestation of your inner being. Your environment is a projection of yourself.

6   When our blocks and inhibitors surface, it is good news because these problems only become visible when the soul knows that we are ready, willing and able to transform them.

7   When clearing your intuitive pool it is important to identify your present situation in terms of your belief system, personality and indeed the reactions of others towards you.

8   Once we have identified the elements that are cluttering our pools, affirm their positive attributes, convert them into strengths, and eliminate any negative energies attached to them. They will then leave us. By eliminating them we are converting negative attributes into positive skills. By changing the face of the problem, the problem is released.

9   In reality there is nothing that is inherently bad or evil, it is only our perception of something that may have no present day use for us.

10   Becoming intuitive defies most established laws of logic because we manifest it via our feelings, not through our intellect. It is through our feelings that intuitive thought is recognised.

11   All truth, by its very nature, stands naked and unashamed to be tested over all experiences of life. It requires no embellishment. It is only through our egoistic attempts to avoid change that we inhibit our happiness, sense of fulfilment and prosperity.

4

W I N T E R

Keeping the Pool Clear

Having identified the clutter in your creative storehouse and forged a will to relax and let go of it, remember the time of winter is:

A time for preparation and a time to plan

A time for reflection and a time of patience

A time for nurturing and a time to regenerate

A time for balance and a time for rest

A time to await the thaw and anticipate the new

Determine to keep all outdated influences from returning to your sphere of creativity.

THE PARABLE OF THE SWIMMING POOL

Have you ever tried to keep the leaves out of a swimming pool?
Many years ago I stayed with a friend who had a large pool. It
sat away from the house amid beautifully landscaped gardens
and trees that towered majestically over it. Naturally the pool's
surface collected its share of leaves, insects and any other
debris that wanted a swim. Because my friend disliked cleaning the pool, I volunteered for the chore. Most mornings I went
down to the pool and cleared it with a long pool net. Maybe it's
because I am a Virgo, but I found that I looked forward to this
time of the day.

There is something relaxing about being close to water. I
found that, while preoccupied with the task on hand, my mind
would wander. Because of the setting I felt one with nature and
allowed myself to philosophise and dream. I would picture
myself as a Chinese sage with a Taoist leaning. By becoming
one with my fantasy I started to search for the meaning of life in
the menial task of pool cleaning. Lao Tse, the father of Taoism
always searched nature for the guides to right action. He could,
by searching out the wisdom in natural laws, obtain great
insight into himself and the human condition. If he could do it,
I thought I could too. So observe I did.

I noticed that when I vigorously skimmed the water's surface
with the pool scoop, the action on the water pushed the leaves
away from me. Certainly I collected some but the rest always
moved out of reach. The wake I created pushed them away.
Hence I reasoned that the first law of pool-clearing was to
approach it calmly and gently.

How could I trap the leaves more efficiently? This puzzled
me until one day I noticed that as the wind blew across the
surface the leaves, if left alone, gathered in certain parts of the
pool. All I had to do on windy days was to wait until the wind
rounded up enough leaves for me to scoop gently them out.

Law two of pool-clearing emerged. The activity of life will
always assist me in my tasks of clearing. I decided to let life
bring to me the unconscious issues in myself that needed attention instead of running around to find them. A subparagraph of
the second law is to work with the most obvious. When you
think about it, the most obvious is the present moment. I
reasoned that as I dealt with the immediate issues that life

brought my way, the winds would always bring new leaves to me to replace the old. This theory seemed to work yet didn't explain how I was going to retrieve the leaves that had sunk deep down in the pool. These leaves were so far down that the pool pole was not long enough to reach them. I thought about this for some weeks. Every time I visited the pool there were always leaves that I could not reach. One day, after a pool party, I noticed all the sunken leaves bobbing on the surface. What was the difference?

Obviously the activity of the guests in the pool had stirred them up. Law two subsection two surfaced. I don't need to dive deep into the pool to clear out the leaves at the bottom. I only need to allow the interaction with others to bring deep-seated issues into consciousness. Personal relationships are a magnificent way to work on ourselves.

Assuming the role, again, of the Chinese sage I advised myself that the most effective way of clearing out my unwanted beliefs was to do it with a minimum of fuss. Trust the processes of life. Take personal responsibility to act on the issues in my life that presented to me now.

There were times when I thought that I had taken all the debris out of the pool only to find that another gust of wind blew more in. I was quite angry about this. Sometimes the anger and frustration turned to despondency and I wondered why I bothered. I asked my imaginary Chinese sage how to resolve this problem. The answer that came back to Bruce, the student, wasn't what I wanted to hear. The sage said to me that it was my expectations that caused my anger and frustration. He said that I expected that I would reach a stage when I could finish with clearing. I had to admit that this was true. He reasoned with me that my attitude was nonsensical. The process of clearing was simply the integrating of experiences that I no longer had use for. In other words, I had learnt from my experiences. If I wanted to stop clearing, he said, that implied that I wanted to stop experiencing. This reluctance to experience life suggested that I wanted to opt out of life altogether. Let go of my resistance to life, he said. Let go of my expectations and change my attitude!

Let's go back to the beginning. At first, when I removed the leaves, I wanted to do something useful with them. Being quite the conservationist, I deposited the dead leaves on the garden for mulch. Some time later, however, I noticed that some shrubs looked sick. It was about this time that the gardener turned up. He looked in horror at what he saw. The pool chemicals had contaminated the mulch and were killing the plants. So back I went to the sage. I thought that I had done the right thing. The sage looked at me and smiled tolerantly. What right did I have, he asked, to put my stuff on someone else without their consent. If my beliefs proved outdated for me, why did I think that they could benefit anyone else?

So, law three of pool clearing, came about. Don't push my opinions down someone else's throat. My experiences are for my benefit. Your experiences are for your benefit. We can intellectualise and listen to another's experiences. Yet until we experience the advice for ourselves, it could mislead us.

THE BENEFITS OF ANALOGY AND IMAGERY

By now, you probably can see the benefits of using analogies to bring out intuitive thought. Intuition works when we detach ourselves from the obvious and take a sideways look at the subject. Imagery also helps; I started by imagining a Chinese sage. I told my intellect that it was all right to fantasise like this. Then I began talking to it as if it was real. The conversations that I had with this other part of me had wisdom in them. By displacing the linear intellectual face of my ego, I stepped sideways into another dimension altogether. This act allowed me to reach my intuition and communicate with the soul.

Crazy as it sounds, think about all the times you have conversations in your head. Many clients have told me that this occurs when they drive. Whenever it happens to you, I guarantee that it will happen when you are alone and doing something else. Clearing the intuitive pool is a job best done alone. Interaction with others, however, can certainly provide the stimuli.

EFFORTLESS PERFECTION

It is through our experiences and relationships that our growth accelerates. We all work towards advancement of some kind. One way to advance is to heal our hurts and reorient our false beliefs, all of which occur in the linear reality of the ego. Life patterns do surface that require releasing so that change can happen for us. These patterns can stand in the way of clear intuitive thought. Usually when we live in the linear reality, our egos waste considerable amounts of energy on useless goals because they expect outcomes based on experience — the old cause and effect rule.

Such a dogmatic approach forces us to operate solely inside the nine dots. This restricts soul expression and blocks our intuitive processes from accessing the soul because the soul exists in the world of non-attachment. It is in the world of non-attachment that endless opportunities exist.

Life is full of goodness. Yet on the surface it can, at times, appear that the process of clearing is a continual, never-ending drudge. Sometimes we encounter people who become so committed to change that they are constantly introspective. They examine everything in minute detail always looking for the smallest pea under the mattress. These people are striving for perfection and will tell you that they will achieve it even if it kills them. I am sure that sometimes it does. They process themselves tirelessly expecting that the amount of effort expended is directly proportional to their growth.

Admittedly, there are times when we need to work hard because that is what the conditions at the time demand but we must avoid being caught up in the ultimate illusion of linear reality. The illusion is that it takes effort to grow and that where you are now lacks something. Some people live in the illusion of deficit need and stand between themselves, their happiness and fulfilment. Why? Because they believe that perfection is out there somewhere and that they must do something to get it.

Intuitive people take a different stance. They accept that they are perfect now and live in a state of perfection. Everything in their lives is perfect for their growth now and by living intuitively their growth is effortless. As in everything, we have a choice. We can choose the linear method of clearing the pool or the multi-dimensional approach.

In my psychic awareness classes, students come to learn and develop for many reasons. In the initial stages, they all seem to go through this stage of effort. It often seems that we only need to try hard to obtain something that we don't have. We are all spiritual beings and indeed we are all intuitive. Therefore, all we need to do to let our blocks surface is to sit back and let it happen. That's right! To develop intuitively we must take on the role of the dispassionate observer.

Many students sit in the class with perfect intention. I can feel them straining in the silence of meditation to 'become psychic'. Sometimes this attitude of effort will last for well over two years. Then, in a moment of time, the student knows that they are psychic. They realise that the very attributes that they have tried to acquire, they have already. Once this realisation occurs, the student's developmental path leaves the horizontal plane and soars skywards.

So why are we talking about clearing and releasing when I am talking about effortlessness? Our lives on this planet and the experiences we have are the catalysts for growth. This is an automatic process. There is no need to go in search of the blocks to our intuition. We need not dive deep into our pools to see what is underneath the surface. We need only to wait at the surface and observe. When the blocks emerge we can choose to lovingly remove them. In so doing, you will let go of the worn-out machinery in your barn and the conditioning that is no longer relevant in your life.

THE BENEFITS OF DETACHMENT

Buddhists understand the benefits of detaching from outcomes. When they meditate, they calmly, effortlessly and from a perspective of disinterested interest, scan their bodies to observe the sensations that arise from within. They observe heat, cold, pain or pleasure, yet they place no interpretations on these sensations. They become the observers of their processes because it is the interpretations that form the attachments. It is the interpretations that the ego requires so that it can judge and remain separate.

Judgement, criticism and evaluation all serve to create the illusion of separateness and support our ego belief system. Our beliefs reside and are created by the ego to form the illusion of safety in the linear world. But our intuitive power does not operate or function through a belief system. Our ego functions by creating beliefs while our soul, our very essence, functions by knowing. Our intuition is a knowing rather than a belief and is an integral part of knowledge — knowing, just is! Intuition just is, and when we can recognise and internalise this idea then we will identify our intuitive guidance.

You will simply know! Reflect on those inexplicable events that occur in your life, and when people ask you how did you know, the reply is 'I don't know, I just knew'! To react to a situation is to attach to it and, in so doing, you lose power. Those who operate and live in 'victim' consciousness, and by that I am referring to those who assume that they are dependent or reliant on others for their happiness, are reactors instead of creators. To be a reactor is to be powerless. To be a creator is to recognise your own creative power and use it.

Intuition is a positive creative force. It is the innovator of action, the wisdom behind all creativity. To the person who believes and acts as a victim, intuition will always remain a vague intangible concept that is beyond reach. These people see intuition as separate from themselves. To acknowledge that we are intuitive internalises the belief, transforming it into knowing, and our ability to intuit expands. A positive affirmation to consolidate this concept is:

I am the perfect creator. I am my intuition. We are one.

Work with this affirmation often. Write it wherever you will see it often and feel its truth.

WINTER IN THE SNOW

Winter time is the time to be introspective, to identify and understand our conditioning. It is the time to clear the debris from our intuitive pools. Reflect for a moment and imagine life during winter in the snow country. You have created the perfect environment inside your house. You have identified, lovingly cleared and transformed those inhibitors into positive aspects. Now you can sit in a warm and comfortable environment filled with love. You feel safe inside your house! You are relaxed and have time on your hands. Yet you sense a void in your life and wonder what to do next. Be aware that your ego is also wondering what has happened. It feels strange and non-separate. It is sitting there looking for outside attitudes and influences that it can relate to and possibly, yearning for the good old days. So when a thought from the outside passes by you and resembles familiar pre-transformed habits, there can be a temptation to reach out and say hello to a once familiar friend and start the cycle again.

During the winter time of release and transformation, be

cautious of the outside winds that are searching for the cracks in your house so they can come into the warmth. Make sure that your house is secure from draughts by simply saying no to these unwanted influences. Deny them a place in your life and give them no weight. Don't expend energy in any attempt to drive away these influences. The moment we give them weight or energy, we have acknowledged and powered them up. Once powered, they will be back into the pool for clearing again.

When a person sits out a raging storm, there is nothing to do except acknowledge its presence and wait for it to pass. This is how we prevent outmoded values from reappearing in our new present. All things change and pass away. Your unwanted influences will behave similarly to the storm that blows hard for a while and leaves. Be content in the knowledge that the storms are cleansing your world and that the inevitable truth is that the sun will shine.

When developing intuition, the winter time is a time to learn patience, to nurture ourselves and to protect the ideas that are crystallising from factors outside ourselves that will inhibit or de-energise our creativity. In any project this is the time for planning and the time to inject life into our plans and goals. By merely embarking upon the intuitive life, we have set in motion an intention on which the soul will act. Our intuition will move closer and closer to the surface. We can inject life into our intuition by meditating upon it, affirming its strength, familiarising ourselves with it and visualising its power. In this germination phase, nothing seems to be happening on the outside, yet it is. Allow yourself to dream, and visualise your intuition functioning in the realities of your everyday life.

THE BENEFITS OF EGO PROJECTION

Up to this point we have placed considerable emphasis on the ego. We have defined the ego as the part of us that acts on information drawn from either linear reality or multi-dimensional reality. The cause and effect scenario is an ego battle and by definition linear; its goals are ultimately control, dominance and separateness. Linear reality is the outward manifestation of ego. The ego acts as a film projector and throws our beliefs onto the screen of life. We view the screen; see ourselves acting on it; become absorbed by it; and believe it to be reality.

Our egos therefore function to show us our inner beliefs in a way that makes them acceptable. Remember that either consciously or unconsciously, we think that we are separate, apart and alone. While this belief exists in us, it will be mirrored in our physical life. Just as a projector will only run one film at a time, so our egos will only project the values and beliefs of the linear world.

To some it may seem easier to look on the ego as some insidious force that compels us to act. Not so! The ego is an obedient servant that merely projects the beliefs of our spiritual personality. It is not separate from us. It is a part of us. It has a function just like the heart, lungs or any other organ of the body. It is the mechanism that will transmit without censorship who we think we are, what we believe, what we think in our deepest most hidden thoughts. How we see the world is how we are. Always remember that. We may try to push reality into our unconscious. We may try to forget unpleasant experiences. But somewhere, somehow, they will manifest in our lives either through contact with others or via physical ailments. Energies that are similar attract each other. It is the same with emotions, for example, if we are angry then we will attract angry people and we will enjoy angry films, songs and stories. If we are kind, we will see kindness all around us and experience kindness from others and so on. Your ego is a treasured part of you that always tells it as it is. Your ego is essential for your survival and growth. Your ego is *you*! Your ego is only a problem when you use it solely in the linear dimension.

Contrary to a popularly held belief, healing takes place in our thoughts rather than our egos. The people we interact with act as mirrors and reflect aspects of our true self. Therefore, when we want to change the world, we are saying to ourselves, that the projection of ourselves is no longer acceptable to us and we wish it to change. To change the world is very simple — just change yourself. If you are a supporter of causes and if you fight for the rights of others and ask others to change, you may be supporting the illusion of separateness and you may be refusing to change yourself.

Intuition can only grow from the positive. Before we plant a seed we need to prepare the ground. Before we dive into our intuitive pools we need to clear them and keep them clear. To develop intuitively, know yourself and be.

WORKSHOP *(allow thirty minutes)*

In life, before healing can occur, we must take the problem that caused the pain back to its original condition to understand it so that we know how to treat it. Scars form as physical, emotional and psychological aberrations to protect us from pain, future hurts and unwanted influences. However sometimes the very scar tissue that is protecting us is also restricting our intuitive flexibility and the growth of our intuitive power. For some, the winter time can prove difficult. If you are one of these people, then I encourage you to persevere at your own pace, and progress through this book when you feel that you are ready.

The chapters in this book are designed so that you can use them in any sequence at any time. For the first reading I suggest that you follow the chapters sequentially. The Nazarene said that a wise person builds a house on solid reliable foundations and a fool builds on sand. To understand and develop our intuition, it is necessary to look at the strength of our foundations and to either reconstruct them or to build upon them. We develop our intuition by recognising reality and emptying ourselves of illusion.

Meditation is an effective method to access those long-forgotten thoughts that still affect our lives. There are many ways to meditate, many purposes for meditation and many opinions on the correct method. However, the function of meditation remains the same. It relaxes our beings and allows us to go within to explore the wonders and marvels of who we are. As you become aware of negative thoughts, emotions and personal laws that are denying your growth, several things may happen for you. For instance:

1   You may experience unpleasant feelings that you had suppressed, for example, hate, embarrassment, rage, resentment and bitterness.
2   You may suddenly remember people and events from your past with similar effects as in point one.
3   You may want to release these thoughts and feelings from your being but something inside you really wants to hold on to them.
4   When you do in fact release them, it may be that more thoughts flood in, and even when you feel free of them,

new circumstances arise that seem to be equally as negative and debilitating.

5   As you release these patterns, life may become a little crazy and unpredictable for a time — view this as good because it is a certain and real sign that growth is occurring.

So understand that, when we start the process of activation, we have begun a journey that is exciting, challenging and satisfying. It's like jumping into the river of life and choosing to flow with it. Observe the scenes on the riverbank as you pass by and rejoice because you are moving onwards to more happiness, satisfaction and fulfilment. The journey inwards through meditative discipline naturally activates our unconscious mind, repressed feelings, thoughts, emotions and attitudes. These then emerge into our conscious minds, or come out in our dreams. The reason they emerge into the conscious part of us is to enable us to evaluate them intelligently and then make choices and decisions about our lives and act on them accordingly. This is the empowerment process.

Always know that we are powerful, creative beings and that we create all things for ourselves, consciously and willingly. To be free of unwanted thoughts acknowledge that they have served your growth positively and then release them. Intuition develops as they are released. So how do we release suppressed beliefs when they become conscious? An example of a good positive release statement is:

I now let go of everybody and everything that I am uncomfortable with.

As you empty your storage tank it behaves like a vacuum. You will notice more thoughts and experiences heading your way to fill it up. This is where discipline and conscious choice are very important. We all have the right to choose our attitudes, beliefs and feelings because we are the gatekeepers of our souls. The most effective way to keep negativity out, is to deny that it can possibly have any effect on us. This way, although it may appear for a time, it will not stay around for long. Remember that we are an outward manifestation of our beliefs and thoughts. Negativity is an illusion and will not affect us unless we acknowledge or allow it to influence us. An example of an effective denial statement is:

No, I do not accept this as reality in my life.

We will now go into the meditation, so find a comfortable position and relax.

Breathe deeply and affirm as you breathe in:

I AM divine love

Exhale and relax more deeply than before. Breathe deeply and affirm as you breathe in:

I AM divine love

Exhale and relax more deeply than before. Breathe deeply and affirm as you breathe in:

I AM divine love

Exhale and relax more deeply than before. Breathe deeply and affirm as you breathe in:

I AM divine love

Exhale and relax more deeply than before.

Now focus your attention at a point on your forehead between your eyebrows and visualise the colour indigo flowing into your body through this point, filling your body with indigo light. As you are relaxing, become aware that you are standing in a magnificent opaque crystal cave. Moonlight is entering the cavern through a crevice in the roof and its rays bounce off the crystal formations. Notice the patterns that the light makes around the cave. This is a place of inspiration and as you begin to float and dance with the rays you feel a strength and determination to succeed like you have never felt before. You feel safe, warm, vibrant and at peace knowing that you are protected. Be one with this experience and for the next twenty minutes dream your plans, foster your determination and feel your success.

You can take this journey as often as you wish. Visualise a beautiful blue light coming down as if it were a shower washing you from head to foot protecting you and centring you now. Notice that you feel relaxed, revitalised and healthy. All is at peace with your soul and you are determined to grow intuitively according to your choices. You have the power to effect positive growth in your life now.

SUMMARY

1   When we act from the linear perspective, we place considerable energy on the attachment of outcomes and expectations. The soul then pulls back into the multi-dimensional world of non-attachment.

2   Intuitive people recognise that they are perfect now and are in exactly the correct moment of their advancement and that their growth is effortless.

3   To be a reactor is to be powerless. To be a creator is to recognise our own creative power and use it positively. Intuition is a positive creative force. It is the innovator of action, the wisdom behind all creativity.

4   During the winter time of release and transformation, be cautious of the outside winds that are searching for any cracks in your house to find a way into the warmth. Make sure that your house is secure from draughts by simply saying no to these unwanted influences and deny that they have any place in your life.

5   By merely embarking upon the intuitive life, we have set in motion an intention on which the soul will act. Our intuition will move closer and closer to the surface.

6   Our egos function to show us our inner beliefs in a way that we can accept.

7   To change the world is very simple — just be willing to change yourself.

8   The development of intuition is enhanced by affirming reality, and we first need to empty ourselves of illusion. Therefore, it may be necessary to look at the strength of your life's foundations and, either, to reconstruct them, if you desire, or to build on them.

9   Meditation is an effective method to access those thoughts which have long been forgotten but nevertheless still have an effect on our lives.

5

Oh! Just Before You Climb the Ladder

The days lengthen. The sun sparks off the ice. A definite freshness arrives. The melting snow creates rivulets of hope.

The momentum of life starts to build. The excitement of the coming spring stirs the soul.

Life changes into small streams that race each other down the mountains. They prepare the soil. They nourish the roots of the growing plant, which is you.

Feel your power. Feel your strength. Feel excited, for these are your last moments in the winter time of this cycle.

Prepare with non-action. Anticipate through non-anticipation. Become excited by the tranquillity. Experience movement in the stillness.

Serenity, peace, contentment and holiness are yours. They are you. Await now with the calm certainty of perfect growth.

THE SKILL IN any creative exercise lies in knowing the order of events; having the foresight to anticipate any consequences; and patiently waiting for the right time to implement your plan. Before beginning any project, set your thoughts and feelings in order.

We stand at the base of the world-championship diving tower. The time will soon be here to begin training, to develop our technique and our physique so that we can produce the perfect dive. We feel excited and become impatient. All we want to do is to just get up there and start practising. The pool is clear. The water is deep and clean. The cross-winds have gone and the sun breaks through the clouds. Until now, all has been theory, speculation and certainly a lot of dreaming. Shortly we will climb the ladder and change our reality. By our own choice, we will accept complete responsibility for our training program. Before taking the next step, pause for a moment, and reflect on the winter time.

We have discussed the elements of the intuitive process. We have related them to the characteristics of the winter time and we've also looked at a farmer who ran out of storage space. Although your intuition may not be clear at this stage, I imagine that somewhere deep inside you there is a spark of knowing which yearns to use your intuition. By meditating upon your intuition, affirming it, reinforcing it, and doing the exercises prescribed, you will have noticed some intuitive thoughts surfacing. If nothing else, there are certainly odd coincidences taking place in your life.

MANAGING CHANGE

Is a strangeness creeping into your life yet? Are friends relating to you differently? By now people whom you have lost contact with over many years will be stopping you in the street or will contact you in other ways. As my students develop there are always certain outward signs in their lives of the inner changes as they happen.

One consistent change is the meeting with past friends and associates. There is not one of my students who hasn't experienced this phenomenon. The people that we draw to us are mirrors to ourselves. They characterise parts of ourselves that our ego wishes us to look at. The winter time of clearing and change provides us with the opportunity to release parts of ourselves that have no more relevance to us. People popping up out of the past give us the opportunities, yet again, to learn from our experiences. Some past acquaintances reappear for a short time only. They present themselves symbolically to us so that we can say goodbye to a part of ourselves that is redundant. Others reappear and stay around for quite a while. These signify issues within us that we suppressed and need to clear. Chance meetings can often spark off a chain of memories long since buried. Whatever the reason, in the winter time, we have yet another opportunity to re-examine our beliefs.

Right now in our quest to become the world-champion high diver, we have cleared the pool, become familiar with it and excited with the prospect of the dive. Our intuition is beginning to grow and we can see that some of our intuitive thoughts are working and others are not.

Every developing intuitive person should remember that it takes the experience gained through time to understand and interpret intuitive thought. Sometimes we act on what we believe to be our intuition and the outcome is not as we expected. It is not an indication that our intuition was wrong. It is showing us that what we believed to be an intuitive thought was, in reality, a thought generated from linear ego desire.

From experience I've found that it takes time and considerable experimentation to fine tune this art. Those who sail will understand it when I say that it takes several attempts to fine tune a yacht on land and many sailing excursions before it is tuned satisfactorily. It is the same with our intuition. There are times when we need to venture into everyday life and put our intuition to the test. Then there are times when we need to retreat, meditate and continue the fine adjustments that are necessary. At this stage, it's the time to retreat, to place your life in order, to allow your intuition to develop.

Ironically while we are reprogramming the ego from the limited linear reality to the multi-dimensional, the logical mind does not expect to go where the soul wants to lead. The temptation is strong, at this time, to look into the future for outcomes to feel secure while the change is happening. This is where people try to use their intuition. Future predictions have a place in the intuitive person's tool kit, for instance, if you have a premonition that your child will run out in front of a bus, then you should act on your intuition. But when you are developing a project, you may unconsciously modify your methods to make your predicted outcome happen. When we want something to happen so much, we risk interpreting an ego statement as intuition.

I frequently have clients come to me with this problem. They look at me disconsolately and say that they chose a particular course of action because they felt so sure that it would create what they wanted. Here is an example. A client, whom I will call Jim, was having a particularly tough time of finding a permanent house to live in. When Jim came to see me he was renting a property that the owner wanted him to vacate. Jim looked around and found a house that was perfect. It was available for long-term rental and had everything that he wanted. Naturally when he put in his application he gave his current landlord as a referee. Although they had their differences in the past, Jim felt that the landlord would give him a good reference to ensure his early departure. Well, you probably have guessed that the landlord gave the worst possible reference. It was so bad that Jim could not go to any estate agent in the district. After several discussions, we went for a walk along the beach, to see if Jim could intuitively find an answer. In the course of our conversation I had a brainwave.

'What's the most positive thing about this situation?' I asked him. 'Well I don't know' he replied, 'The only thing that I know is that no one will rent a property to me in the district.' Jim paused for a moment, then looked at me with a glint in his eye and said, 'If I can't rent does it mean that I should look at buying a property?' This was a very bold statement for Jim to make. The next weekend he and his wife went house-hunting in the same district. That day they found a house that had been vacant for a year. The owners were keen to sell. What's more, he told, me that it was better than he could have imagined. The conclusion of the story is that Jim and his family moved into this new property within ten days of finding it. Our intuition always knows best. If the ego can't visualise opportunities then it is because it is looking at the result based on experiences. The landlord, who at first Jim disliked intensely, actually helped Jim on a soul level to find something more suitable.

PREDICTING THE FUTURE

Looking into the future carries with it the drawback of basing future expectations on past results. It is futile to look further than the present because both the past and the future are irrelevant to what we need to achieve now. When you operate from intuition you can feel blindfolded and out of control because you cannot see the steps into the future. It takes courage to live intuitively and to trust your intuitive knowing.

Remember, we choose to live on this planet for the ultimate development and learning of our souls and we achieve this from our experiences. I once heard of an affable Chinese sage who acted like a simpleton. He often laughed incessantly when teaching his students and spoke in direct, simple language. One of his students came to him because she was experiencing a particularly difficult phase of her development. She needed to make decisions intuitively, which at the time seemed quite illogical. She would from time to time wonder if she was losing all grasp of reason and hence her rational mind. By nature she was impatient and with this attitude she once said to her teacher that she could cope with her lessons if only he would tell her where she was heading. She wanted to assure herself that all this effort was worthwhile. The sage sat on his rock and said to her with great respect, 'If we showed you the goal, then you would avoid looking at your steps and fail to learn. Live now and treasure today's experiences knowing that your development is certain'.

The student never asked him or any of her teachers for an outcome again. You see, by wanting to know the outcome before time she was attached to it and was not concentrating on the means to get there. The knowing that is real is that all outcomes are one hundred per cent correct. There is no other way.

Intuitive people act on their intuition now. They know that the outcomes of their intuitive actions are perfect. The intuitive person does not need to know about the future because it is a dimension that always takes care of itself. If you are in business, imagine acting without forward projections, cost estimates, targets and goals. Your shareholders and associates would quickly become concerned and disenchanted with you. Understand that targets, goals and aspirations are perfectly acceptable provided you change with them when required. We all have read, I'm sure, of people who succeed after experiencing events that at the time appeared catastrophic. For me, my intuitive development began after my car, with me in it, rolled end over end down a twenty-metre embankment. I walked away from the accident unharmed and learnt a lot about trust and protection that night and a little bit about fear as well. Had I known the outcome before the event then the experience would have been worthless to me. The value was in the experience.

In the same way as the accident happened without warning, the outcome or end point of an intuitive thought can occur unexpectedly. Once you can recognise your intuition, always follow it without question. This is the mark of the intuitive person. Should others question you and ask you why, then simply reply that you don't know why but you do know that it is right. In time, as the sceptics around you witness your success, one of two things will happen. Either they will accept your intuitive nature or find others who wish to live in the illusion of negativity and leave you alone.

INTUITION AND TIME MANAGEMENT

At the end of winter the anticipation of spring is in the air. The farmer can feel it, senses it and quite often smells the change. He knows that soon it will be time to start work. Soon it will be time to prepare the soil, to plant and to spend many hours outside in the fields. The wise farmer recognising this will begin to order his life now; mend his tools and prepare for spring. If he doesn't, then when he needs to work long hours, he'll complain that he does not have enough time.

Do you have friends or acquaintances who are always complaining that there are not enough hours in the day? Maybe they should be saying that *they* do not have enough hours in the day. Order your life in preparation for the spring time of your intuitive development. We would not climb the ladder for our world-championship dive in a dinner suit, and we should not dive into our intuition improperly attired. For intuition to develop, we need to order our lives across mind, body and affairs. When there is disharmony in your life, begin to order yourself from within. That's right. Order starts inside us and is initially an emotional quality.

Catherine Ponder in her book *The Healing Secrets of the Ages*, a book that every intuitive person will benefit from reading says, 'Order works through emotional harmony. Order that is achieved without harmonious emotional order is not order, it is conflict and leads not to order but to confusion' (p. 200). To this end we must individually formulate our own scheme of order. Winter is a time for preparation and planning. We need to direct activities inward, knowing that outward activity will occur when the season changes. Our intuition requires a peaceful, contented and ordered environment to grow. Now is the time to eliminate those emotions that have created the illusion of blocks in our intuitive pools. Now is the time when it is imperative to accentuate the positive, dissolve the negative and clear the way for our intuition to surface.

UNDERSTANDING YOUR INTUITION

Oh, just before you climb the ladder! Have you cleared the pool? Have you established a training schedule? Have you selected a training squad? Decided what dives to learn? Have you selected your coach?

You see, as we glimpse something new and exciting we naturally want to use it straight away. Suppose I drove the latest Porsche into your driveway and handed you the keys. Then said that it was yours. You possibly would want to sit behind the steering wheel, put the keys in the ignition and head towards the nearest motorway. Once on the freeway, powering the car over the 160 km mark, would you then look around the cabin, adjust the mirrors, tune the radio and familiarise yourself with all its options? It could be a little dangerous. It is better to familiarise yourself with the car before you test its full potential.

It is the same with intuitive thought because, firstly, the intuitive process is intangible. It is also fragile. For you to function effectively with your intuition, you must use it confidently, without question, and understand its performance specifications. If we were to take our intuition out of the garage, power it up to its full potential, without first understanding it, then we may lose control and have a collision with, in this case an ego block. We may then be reluctant to get back into the car and drive it again. Intuition is a tool of a confident person who knows the extent to which intuition is usable. Should you venture out too early and come to grief, you may become disillusioned and hesitant. After an experience like this some people are disinclined to use their intuitive power for a long time.

In any psychic awareness class there is usually one person who acts from impulse hoping that the impulse is intuitive. If they are fortunate, when they hit an ego block they will talk to someone in the group. Be encouraged. Understand the problem, go back to basics and continue to develop. For some, however, the magnitude of their disillusionment is too great and they never return.

THE INTUITIVE SUPPORT GROUP

When beginning anything new it is important to find a training or support squad that best suits you. The ultimate goal of the intuitive person is to be totally reliant on the intuitive process. Similarly, when it is time to dive competitively, we are the only one making the dive. Getting there, however, can be trying and difficult without support. To work in a group training situation is vital when the going gets tough. It is inspiring when you witness the courage and progress shown by your peers. Most of all, you will benefit from the positive energy generated from such a group. The features to look for in a support group are:

1   Non-judgemental acceptance.
2   A positive energy evidenced by happiness and love within the group.
3   The dedication of each member to a single purpose and one hundred per cent commitment to developing his or her abilities.
4   An attitude of respect between group members for the individual's right of choice and life's purpose.
5   A teacher who recognises the value of support and encouragement and uses him- or herself as a catalyst and as a source of experiential research to draw upon when required.

You should avoid any teacher or person who teaches you that their way is the only way. In reality, the way you develop and the methodology you develop is uniquely yours and has value only for yourself. A wise teacher will recognise this and teach by not teaching. An excellent teacher will already be an intuitive leader. Your ultimate coach is the soul. Before diving into your intuition, even before putting one foot on the ladder, it is important to find your coach.

WORKSHOP (allow one hour)

We are going to meditate again. Go to that comfortable place that by now you are very familiar with. The meditation will take about twenty minutes. Allow another half an hour at least to write down any ideas arising from the meditation that relate to ordering your life.

Breathe deeply and affirm as you breathe in:

I AM divine love

Exhale and relax more deeply than before. Breathe deeply and affirm as you breathe in:

I AM divine love

Exhale and relax more deeply than before. Breathe deeply and affirm as you breathe in:

I AM divine love

Exhale and relax more deeply than before. Breathe deeply and affirm as you breathe in:

I AM divine love

Exhale and relax more deeply than before.

Now focus your attention on your solar plexus. Visualise two separate streams of light connecting you to the universe. These colours are orange and yellow. Know that the purpose of the meditation is to realign your world and affairs in an orderly fashion.

Relax more deeply and feel your thoughts leaving the body. Now follow the orange and yellow rays high up into the sky until you find yourself in a classroom. At the end of the classroom is a large movie screen with a comfortable lounge chair to sit in and view the screen. You feel relaxed and start to watch the screen. This screen is the intelligent part of you that will show you objectively how to bring your world into order.

Relax now, witness the pictures and later write down what you saw on the screen.

When it is time to finish the meditation, visualise the blue light wrapping you up from head to foot and note that you feel healthier and more intuitive than you ever have before.

Spend the next thirty minutes recording your plan of action in a work book.

SUMMARY

1   When we act on our intuition and the outcome is not as we expected, it may be that our interpretation of the intuitive thought may, in reality, have been a thought generated from our ego.

2   One aspect of our soul is that it can lead us, via our intuition, to places where our logical minds do not expect to go.

3   The only knowing that is real is that all outcomes are one hundred per cent positive. There is no other way. Once you can recognise your intuition, always follow it without question. This is the mark of the intuitive person.

4   Our intuition requires a peaceful, contented and ordered environment to grow.

5   Your intuitive growth and the methodology you develop is uniquely yours and has value only for yourself.

6   People that we draw around us are mirrors to ourselves. They represent parts of our inner being that our ego wishes us to look at.

7   Every developing intuitive person should remember that it takes the experience gained through time to understand and interpret intuitive thought.

8   Looking into the future carries with it the drawback of basing future expectations on past results.

9   For you to function effectively with your intuition, you must use it confidently, without question, and understand its performance specifications.

10   Your ultimate coach is the soul. Before diving into your intuition, even before putting one foot on the ladder, it is important to find your coach.

6

A Time to Grow Your Intuition

Each birthday is a celebration of possibilities

Each birthday is filled with love

Each birthday shows an increase of wisdom

Each birthday is exciting in its newness

May your path be light under your feet and the forest through which you walk be fresh and alive with possibilities, filled with love.

A ND SO THE excitement of spring is upon us. This is the season where the intuitive seed breaks open and the tender shoots push into the outer world. By the end of winter we have completed the stages of clearing, evaluating and measuring effectiveness, idea generation and planning for the success of our project. Now in spring we look around us and witness the gestation that took place.

Here we see the first outward signs that life was growing in the hidden, inner realms of ourselves during the winter time. Fruit trees burst into blossom and wait for cross-pollination to occur. Newborn lambs leap for joy as they learn to use their muscles and to test their environment, while the elders watch them and remember their youth.

When the spring time bursts into the cycle the newborn display a fresh naivety. For the young, it is a time of simplicity and a time of freedom. They are exploratory. They are fearless. They expect goodness at all times. They refuse to see any danger. They trust in their guardians. They know that they will be fed. Their naive innocence is inspirational.

The experienced farmer has lived through many seasons and knows that this innocence will attract predators looking for an easy kill. These predators delight in the first moments of spring because it heralds the end of lean winter hunts.

When our intuition emerges, it is fresh and exciting both to ourselves and to others. Yet with it comes danger from those who live in the linear world and who refuse to take responsibility for their decisions. Spring time inspires us to play with our intuition and indeed we should. Do be careful though not to become blasé and forget to protect your delicate new talent.

Have you experienced the child who, innately, knows the truth behind people's actions and with absolute innocence tells them how it is? When my daughter was a preschooler, it was as though I had a wise old soul there questioning, commenting on my actions and making observations with stunning clarity and accuracy. I remember, only too well, my reactions to her fresh honest openness and the way I would draw back from her when the truth struck too close to the mark. I would try to suppress her openness when, in the presence of a group, she would tell it how it was, because 'it was impolite'. I am sure most readers have experienced similar situations with young children.

Society has developed rules of conduct to suppress open honest expression. Have you noticed, as children grow older, that a certain self-consciousness creeps in when the values of parents, relatives and peers start to overlay the child's expression about who he or she is? Children adapt their behaviour to fit in and, in so doing, repress open soul expression. It is this modification process that creates the linear world of restriction. Distortion of reality begins. Ultimately we grown children have unlearned the ability to express ourselves as we truly feel. As a result, emotional conditions set in that radically affect behaviour, health and happiness. Western health facilities thrive on this process and psychiatrists, psychologists and counsellors flourish in successful practices because of it.

Children observe from their souls before this conditioning process takes place. Intuition is natural for them. Dominance, competition and control are the products created by the suppression of their intuitive expression.

During winter time, we focused on identifying and releasing the blocks to intuition created by the ego. These blocks resulted from our acceptance of the controls that society placed on us. At the start of spring, our intuition emerges again as fresh, innocent and above all very accurate. It is also vulnerable to others who, because of their own reluctance to move away from linear thought, avoid the reality of the multi-dimensional world and hence the notion of change.

Victims live in a state of denial and foster illusory conditions to avoid personal responsibility for the outcomes of the choices that they make. Intuitive people by comparison consciously make choices, act upon them and accept the results as positive experiences. The intuitive person is the creator of destiny. The victim is the reactor to self-illusion.

The irony is, of course, that we are all creators, whether it be the creator of reality or of illusion and the victim is as powerful a creator as the intuitive person, yet doesn't know it. If I had my parenting time again, I would approach the intuitive development of my daughter differently. I would encourage her intuitive outbursts. I could show her when she was reacting to ego illusion and encourage her to act on her intuitions without apology. I would gently direct her into the company of other intuitives to provide the most suitable environment for her intuition to grow.

Fortunately there is no end to infinity. We can always begin again to create positive change in our lives. Spring time is the time to recognise our intuitions, honour them and dedicate ourselves to growing them. At this time in our development the entire energy of the seasons will support us and inspire us to nurture our intuitive child.

Love it, respect it, laugh with it, play with it, grow with it, protect it, encourage it and you will know it better.

SUMMARY

1   Spring is the season where the intuitive seed breaks open and the tender intuitive expressions push into the outer world.

2   As our intuition emerges, it is fresh and exciting both to ourselves and to others. Yet with it comes danger from those who live in the linear world of illusion and who do not wish to take responsibility for their own decisions.

3   The intuitive person is the creator of destiny. The victim is the reactor to self-illusion.

4   At this time in our development the entire energy of the season supports us and inspires us to nurture our intuitive child.

5   In life through the seasons and cycles there is time for growth, time for rest, time for activity and time for reflection. Now is the time of intuitive growth for you. Trust that the understanding will come later on.

7

S P R I N G

Let's Do Some Warm-up Exercises

The flame of life, nurtured beneath the snow, bursts forth again, flickering, dancing, energising and inspiring in its celebration.

Seeds, plants and trees push towards the sun, the buds of their potential swell with pride, life, procreation and re-creation. Indeed all forms of life respond to the excitement of this time.

This is a time to show beauty, to receive warmth, to be nourished and to give pleasure.

Celebrate life, celebrate growth, be energised, be inspired, be creative.

At THE BEGINNING of any project, fresh ideas require nurturing. It's the beginning of spring and it's the time to start training.

In winter the seed lies asleep while it waits for spring to inject life into it. Similarly our intuition quietly rests within us while it waits for us to spark it into life. Although in winter we know that it is a part of us, we rarely experience external proof of its might and power. Yet the intuitive seed has roots deep in our soul.

INTUITIVE SPIRITUALITY

To recognise and bring our intuition to life, we must acknowledge its spiritual nature. In so doing we must also acknowledge our own spirituality. Spirituality has many definitions when translated through the experiential filters of life. The definition of spirituality here refers to the creative energy of the soul. Therefore everything your soul chooses to undertake is spiritual. You are a spiritual being. You are by your very nature and definition spiritual.

Spirituality is the expression of your creative spirit. It is without religious connotations. Some organised groups attempt to program people in specific modes of behaviour and this endangers soul expression. Soul expression is multi-dimensional whereas group expression through dogma and law is linear. The first opens the individual to infinite opportunities. The later restricts the individual's right of expression. It suppresses soul-motivated creativity.

Your creativity is within you and is you. Your spiritual development involves every experience in your entire life. You are an integral part of universal love and cannot separate yourself from it. Spirituality just is. Should you feel separate from it then you have created the illusion of aloneness. Feeling alone is a tendency of the splintered personality. There are many things that just are. It is important to list some of them now.

1   You are *a part of* soul. You are not *apart* from soul.
2   You are one with every aspect, personality and energy of soul.
3   You are complete.
4   You are expansive.
5   You are creative.

6 You are love. You are loved. You are a lover of everything.
7 You are spiritual.
8 You are.

I cannot write about you separately because we are all one.
This is the I AM THAT I AM. You are the I AM, I am the I AM,
and we are the I AM. That is why affirmations beginning with I
AM are all expansive. They are by their very nature acknowl-
edging the power of God.

SOUL-PROJECTED PERSONALITIES

The notion of separateness is an illusion necessary for your
soul to grow. Your soul splits off a part of itself and forms your
personality that carries with it the illusion of separateness. Yet
deep inside your soul is the knowing that it is one with everything. This notion manifests itself by creating the drive for
unity. The desire for external unity is the ego drive to reunite
with the soul. The illusion of separateness is vital for the soul's
expansion because it is through this reuniting process that we
learn from our experiences. It's like a pendulum swinging.

At one extreme is the illusion of separateness. At the other
extreme is the belief that wholeness is somewhere far away
from us and that we should seek it out. The swinging movement of the pendulum from one extreme to the other generates
our experiences. When we integrate our experiential learning
into the archives of the soul, then the energy moving the pendulum recedes until at some point it comes to rest and is still.
This is the moment when transformation occurs. This is the
moment of creative power. This is when the soul expands itself
and creates the next experiential swing of the pendulum. It is in
this stillness, at the very precise moment of peace that the
communication channels open to the entire universe and your
intuition becomes absolute. It is not surprising then, that the
Nazarene said 'Be still and know that I AM God'. When we are
still and know that we are God, we ignite the intuitive seed
within us and spring time starts.

This is not a one-off event. Remember that the soul creates
the pendulum movement through illusion and that these pendulum swings are essential for our growth. There are many
moments of absolute peace and stillness. We all can achieve
them. Once we have mastered the art of stillness in meditation,

we can speak with our soul anywhere and at any time. It is in the stillness that our ego can hear our intuition. Intuition is the language of the soul. Stillness is a created thought just like anything else. This stillness is the ground in which to plant your intuitive seed. This stillness is where you can and will begin all your soulful creations.

FINDING THE SILENCE

We are training to become the world-champion high diver. Have you ever watched champion divers standing at the platform's edge just before their dive? They assume a pose of complete stillness in body, mind and emotions. Then wait for the energy surge. In other words, at this moment the divers are accessing the knowledge required from the soul to make the dive. They are opening the gate that leads into the stillness. And following this split second of stillness they make a world class dive. Athletes who seriously try to extend their limits, all do this. We see it so often in a close tennis match. A player who is about to lose comes to the final serve, pauses, finds the stillness and serves an ace. The game changes, the player ultimately wins and the critics refer to this moment as the moment when 'the player found that something extra'. What the player found was the silence. Watch successful athletes moments before their record-breaking feats and you will see them find the silence.

Our warm-up exercises are simply practising to find the silence when and where we want to. Meditation is an excellent starting point when practised in a controlled environment. It will give you the opportunity to experience the stillness no matter how brief it is. There are many techniques that we can use to reach the stillness. There are also many signs that tell us we are in it. For each person these signs are different. It is up to you to discover them for yourself.

In my experience of stillness I become aware of an overwhelming sense of peace and lightness of body. Sometimes a drowsiness surrounds me and my body tingles with a sensation that feels like a very warm, fine vibration. At these times I am aware of my intuitive insights. The signals are subtle so it is necessary to stay alert to recognise them; otherwise an ego desire may be interpreted as intuition. Intuitive flashes come from the soul. Your desires are a part of your personality. To identify a desire as an intuitive flash and then act on it can be misleading.

HUNCHING

Acting on your hunches is the key to developing your intuition. Remember how young animals play and explore their environment. Sometimes they come to grief or so we think. But there is nothing that is a mistake. Experiences that do not turn out the way we expect are valuable because they teach us what is intuition and what is not. Do not feel disillusioned if you believe your intuition was wrong and don't be afraid to try again. The chances are that your intuition was not evident and that it was an ego desire.

Ego desire and expectation are twins. They are not related to intuition. Intuitive thought is a knowing. It will not justify itself. Neither will it attach to outcomes. Intuitive thought recognises the soul's wisdom and lives in complete trust knowing the perfection of the source.

THE DANGER OF RITUAL

I must caution you at this stage. We are all programmable beings and love to rely on form and ritual. I sometimes see this among psychic colleagues and students. I am sure that they see it in me too. We love to be theatrical, dramatic and grand. We invent rituals to help us achieve certain states of being. When meditating, for example, it is possible to condition ourselves to particular forms of music so that we come to believe (notice that belief creates the illusion) that the music is responsible for us achieving the meditative state. It is very easy to transfer our power to outside factors and, if this happens, we may find it difficult to meditate when conditions change.

When we use techniques it is important to change them when they become ritualised. I am sure that you wish to be able to use your intuition when and wherever you want to. The belief that you must meditate in a certain place, at a certain time and to certain music will seriously hamper your ability to do this. If nothing else, it's quite inconvenient. Allow yourself to let go of any techniques that have become ritualised. Holding on to past methods because we feel comfortable with them will only slow us down. Remember the farmer and the cluttered barn.

INTUITIVE ENTHUSIASM

Have you ever experienced uncontrollable excitement when you have a new idea? This euphoric state lasts for a while. We feel lighter, happier and more optimistic. We feel that nothing can fail and that the idea is infallible.

As the idea grows, so does our enthusiasm. Our minds run wild with the fantasy of success, creating more ideas, more possibilities and more favourable results. If allowed to run unchecked, this process can continue until the seed turns into a tree that has outgrown our world and is looking to take over the universe. Expansionism is excellent. Remember that our thoughts create our reality, so the generation of positive vibes can only be beneficial.

The Nazarene once used the imagery of a mustard seed to explain the limitless nature of creative thought. He said that when we compare the size of the seed (the inspiration of life) to the size of the mature tree (the outcome of growth) it is illogical to explain the transformation of the seed into a tree by deductive reasoning the (linear perspective). In nature we see examples of this everywhere. Caterpillars and butterflies are so different it is almost impossible to believe that such a transformation can take place. To look at a drop of water and speculate about its potential as atomic power is just as preposterous.

There are infinite possibilities in every speck of intelligent thought. These possibilities will generate amazing results. Similarly, there are many touches of brilliance that never reach their potential because they are out of phase with the seasons. When we draw our ideas from the soul, the possibilities are boundless. They know no restriction because they are multi-dimensional. Our personality expresses itself in the physical world where we can create tangible benefits in the linear sense. To work with our intuition, we must recognise this fact and arrange our affairs so that the two universes are in balance and in harmony.

Consider the difference between *wants* and *needs*. Wants are desires of the personality to satify the ego drive for emotional fulfilment. Needs are tangible tools that we require to allow creative expression to emerge from the soul. Wants are linear in nature and needs are multi-dimensional. Effective intuitive expression is a matter of perspective and aligning the two realities.

THE WANT MODEL

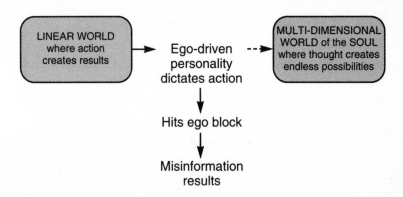

Diagram 6 — Strong ego desires break communication between the linear world and the multi-dimensional world.

THE NEED MODEL

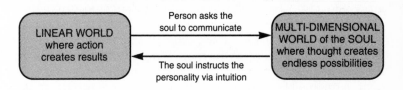

Diagram 7 — Positive results are created when the ego communicates with the multi-dimensional world.

Your soul will always know what you need to grow in the physical world. In the NEED model, the soul drives the personality. In the WANT model, it is the ego belief system of the linear model that drives your personality. The soul will provide for its needs according to the stage or season that your personality is in. It's all about timing.

REACHING FOR YOUR POTENTIAL

How often have you listened to a brilliant idea and then watched it peter out, only to realise its full potential later under different circumstances? The originator of the idea will say that it was perfect but the timing wasn't right. In the spring time, ideas burst into our consciousness like blossoms on a plum tree. If we try to reap the benefits from ideas before growing them according to the seasons they will be premature. The result will be far less than the potential. This is a time to exercise the patience that we learnt in winter. If left alone an idea will grow to its full potential because it was planted in the multi-dimensional soil. The energy of total possibilities will develop it. As our intuition buds, we will see how beautiful it is.

The multi-dimensional person seeks the experiences of life with a passion. 'Mustard seeds' sent from the universal source of wisdom will, if planted in the linear world, serve a different purpose to those planted in the multi-dimensional world.

When we plant the mustard seed in the linear world it will grow into a tree that will project the ego characteristics of our splintered personality. Change is inevitable as we recognise those areas of our lives that are illusory and separate us from the peace and harmony of the multi-dimensional world. When the mustard seed is planted in the multi-dimensional soil, it will bear permanent fruits of a soul nature. In other words the fruits of the seed planted in the multi-dimensional universe are the attributes and qualities of life. The fruits from the seed planted in the linear soil are the outcomes and results.

Outcomes and results are important for us because we live in the linear environment. We must realise that because outcomes are linear they are impermanent. They are transient just like any crop that grows within the earth's seasonal environment. If we become attached to these outcomes we foster a dependence on the external projections of the self. Projections that, by their very nature, are destined to change as we grow.

There are many examples of these projections in the western world today. For instance, people rely on superannuation policies and health schemes, and usually want to be part of a corporation, society or social group because this makes them feel secure.

Popular attitudes towards insurance policies exemplify the individual's denial of his or her own personal power and hence personal responsibilities. For example, by taking out a super-annuation policy in the belief that at a certain age you will be incapable of earning an income is denying your innate power of regeneration. Such people on retiring, accept lump sums, hold on to them and live off a limited income flow and wait to die. If you think that I'm over-dramatising look at the statistics relating to early death after retirement from the workforce.

If people view insurance superannuation from the perspective of actively investing monies earned so that they can generate more income in some future now then they are affirming their resources and expanding on them. When insurance companies take on the responsibilities of others, this burden will eventually grow so large that it will overwhelm them and they will collapse under the weight of the transferred responsibility.

A seed planted in linear soil may produce a restrictive outcome. People become victims to outside circumstances. Yet when they choose to accept responsibility and plant the seed in the multi-dimensional soil they recognise their innate power to create abundantly. This process of recognition affirms growth potential in all stages of life. The insurance policy is a seed that will bear fruit sometimes.

Dependence on external ego projections, together with energy spent on reinforcing and affirming this dependence, creates a separateness from the universal flow of life. Disease manifests because the individual resists moving with the soul's purpose. This is the result of attaching to outcomes. To plant the seed according to the soul's purpose will generate abundant quality of life. When we bring ourselves into alignment with our soul's purpose, disease becomes an illusion and fades away. Happiness, prosperity and fulfilment are all fruits from the seeds planted according to our soul's purpose.

Intuition is the perfect bridge to the multi-dimensional universe that is rich in experience and positive vibes. It is by our intuition, that we find our soul's purpose. Fulfilment is created by aligning with the soul.

WORKSHOP *(allow one hour)*

The seed of intuition is in us. We can choose to apply it to either reality. It is innate, a part of our essence and hence our spirituality. It is our connection to the universal totality of knowledge. Our present environment is the perfect planting ground for our intuitive seed. In the preceding chapters we weeded the soil by consciously transforming aspects of ourselves no longer useful to us. We used our will to prepare the ground. We ordered our environment, both inner and outer, to allow our intuition to grow.

In the early days of my intuitive development, I set aside specific times to sit in meditation and wait for my intuition to speak to me. It was a very special time for me. Sometimes nothing would happen. Sometimes my intuitions would come and when they did I wrote them down. I would leave them alone, sometimes for up to a year, and come back to them when I felt it was time. Any intuitive thought must stand on its own truth. Sometimes information comes intuitively that is for some future now. I would write whatever came through, never sharing the information with anyone until I had identified the source as either an ego projection or from the soul. This book is a result of intuitive comment that started in December 1990.

At the time of writing the information it felt good yet had seemingly little application in my world then. This is often how intuition first appears to us until we can understand it and ourselves.

Now it is the time to start the warm-up exercises to prepare our intuitive bodies for the world-championship dive. These warm-up exercises will strengthen our intuitive muscle, develop intuitive flexibility and generate greater vitality in your life. While in training, we use love as the intuitive weights program. We may think of love as intangible but to use intuition pragmatically, the energy of love is imperative. Again the first exercise is a guided meditation, so relax, allow yourself thirty minutes for the meditation and thirty minutes writing time afterward. When you write this time, allow your hand to put the words on the paper without censorship so that your intuition will give you the information relevant to you at this time.

EXERCISE

Assume a comfortable position and relax.

Breathe deeply and affirm as you breathe in:

I AM divine love

Exhale and relax more deeply than before. Breathe deeply and affirm as you breathe in:

I AM divine love

Exhale and relax more deeply than before. Breathe deeply and affirm as you breathe in:

I AM divine love

Exhale and relax more deeply than before. Breathe deeply and affirm as you breathe in:

I AM divine love

Exhale and relax more deeply than before.

See yourself standing in a green field with lush green trees growing as far as your eyes can see. Feel the warmth of this place and focus on the position in your body where your heart is. See a variety of beautiful vibrant green rays flooding into your being taking you deeper and deeper into your meditative state. Allow yourself to follow the green rays wherever they wish to take you and enjoy the next thirty minutes of meditation. As you come out of your meditation affirm that:

I am divine love. My life is complete and my intuition is manifesting now.

Take some time to absorb the meditation and begin to write — free flow. When you have completed the exercise, wrap yourself completely in a mist of blue light.

FIELDWORK (time allowed: unlimited)

There is no time limit to this exercise because you should incorporate it in your daily regime.

1   Each day on waking ask for divine love to manifest in your life now.

2   Each evening record in your work book all the ways that it manifested during your daily routine.

SUMMARY

1   In winter the seed lies asleep while it waits for the energies of spring to inject life into it. Similarly our intuition quietly rests within us while it waits for us to spark it into life.

2   In order to recognise and use our intuitive energy, we first must acknowledge its spiritual nature and hence our own spirituality.

3   Spirituality is the state that we are in and should not be confused with religious dogma.

4   You are an integral part of universal love and cannot separate yourself from it.

5   The illusion of separateness is vital for the soul's expansion because it is through the reuniting process that we learn from our experiences.

6   When experiential learning is integrated into the archives of the soul, then the energy moving the experiential pendulum recedes until it comes to rest and is still. This is the moment when transformation occurs. This is the moment of creative power.

7   Stillness is a created thought.

8   We warm up by practising to find the silence when we want and where we want it.

9   To identify a desire incorrectly as an intuitive flash and then act upon it can have negative consequences.

10   When we are using meditation, it is important to change the ritual.

11   There are infinite possibilities in every speck of intelligent thought that will generate, given the optimum conditions, amazing results.

12   Dependence on external ego projections, together with energy spent on reinforcing and affirming this dependence, creates a separateness from the universal flow of life.

13   Happiness, prosperity and fulfilment are all fruits from the seeds planted according to our soul's purpose.

14   Intuition is the perfect bridge to the multi-dimensional universe, rich in experience. It is via our intuition that we find our soul's purpose and recognise fulfilment.

8

Intuitive Playtime

Have you heard about the farmer who wanted his plants to grow so much that he snuck out at night and tugged at the new shoots?

Your plans and ideas require time to take root. Allow the intuitive plant to grow unimpeded and enjoy the pleasures of spring. The spring time is:

A time to be young and a time to play

A time to nourish and a time to grow

A time to celebrate and a time to inspire

A time to plant and a time to bloom

A time to manifest and a time to express.

When you have finished the planting and you want to do some more,

PLEASE DON'T!

INJECT LIFE INTO YOUR INTUITION

As our ego blocks clear, our intuition comes closer to the surface. When a project is in the spring phase we can feel the potential of our ideas. Our intuition senses future possibilities and future options. Your ego is learning how to relate to a new set of circumstances and, because it is unsure of future directions, it tries to straddle the old and the new. Remember that your ego is charged with your survival and that your ego-driven self will feel safer if it can see down the road, around the bends and into the distance. It is possible now for your ego to tap into your intuition as it rises to the surface of your intuitive pool. And of course your ego wants to become familiar with our intuitive side because it thinks that if it can predict the future then it can keep us safe.

The danger in using intuition this way, is that we can become obsessed with predicting the future and forget to live in the present. We can use our intuition to focus on outcomes and not on the process. If we choose this path, then we plant our intuition in the linear soil that, by definition, prevents it from communicating with the soul. The ego often takes the easy option. When it thinks that it can get us somewhere quicker and with less effort, then it will. It is easy to fall into this linear trap and to get excited about something that hasn't, yet, realised its full potential. When we focus on results by trying to pick them before they ripen then we will destroy the potential harvest.

The spring time is all about potential. It is not about harvesting. Focusing on potential results is inspirational when we want encouragement along the way. But resting on your laurels without putting in the necessary effort will almost certainly produce disastrous results. There is a difference between the dreamer and the creator. Creators dream and work to bring their dreams to reality. The dreamer dreams, dreams and dreams and dreams.

Love is the fertiliser for our intuitive growth. Now it is the time to inject life into your project. As we glimpse the new life that living intuitively brings, your plans and ideas crystallise into tangible form. This is a time of excitement and a time of hope. A time when we begin to see infinite possibilities. Your project is your creation. It has been born from an idea generated from within you. It is, if you like, your baby, your newborn. For your project to grow, love it, love it and love it some more.

When parents reflect on the first moments of their children's lives, they will tell us that their children were so perfect, innocent, and full of potential. When you hold a baby in your arms, notice its total trust in you. It is the same with any idea that is born. You are totally responsible for your ideas. You must trust your intuition and take care of it and develop it. Intuition is born and grown in love. Love is the basis of all life. Love is the multi-dimensional environment. By planting your intuition in this dimension you give it total intelligence and possibility. It is here that the life force will flow into your intuition filling it with energy.

CROSSING THE BORDER

In the spring time we are presented with many opportunities. Predictions about the future and other sensory phenomena emerge. They risk misinterpretation because we are unfamiliar with them. At this stage of our intuitive development, we are drawing from the multi-dimensional world of infinite possibilities. This is a world that does not attach to or anticipate outcomes.

The multi-dimensional soul is unconditional in nature. It is without condition. In the world of linear thought, words have great power. In the Western world we think that it is better to have security than to be without it. This is where attachment to external accoutrements can cause emotional distress, particularly when we consider that we may lose them. You have a strong ego drive for self-protection. Your ego tries to maintain the status quo and will resist change into the unconditional world of without.

Now, as the life force is surging into consciousness, the ego will project our linear belief system onto the screen of life. It does this to show us the reality that we are leaving behind. Experiences and relationships with others will now reflect our deepest, most hidden beliefs, thoughts and attitudes. Not surprisingly, life, at this time, can go a little crazy. The theory is that having worked through the winter and transformed your negative ego blocks you will attract encouragement, tolerance and acceptance from others. Yet few reach this state in the initial stages. Should you have beliefs that are linear in nature your ego will show them to you on your screen of life usually by the way others relate to you. People who criticise you, for example, usually want you to stay who you were. They will, by their actions, show you your resistance to change. They will refuse to recognise who you are now or the possibility of the person that you can develop into. By witnessing your growth they know that to keep pace with you they will have to change. Chances are they just don't want to do that!

SELECTING YOUR COACH

You will find that people who recognise your talents will start to give you advice. Some of the advice will prove fruitful and some of it misleading. These are the spring games. They provide an arena for you to play in and use your intuition to decipher which advice is valuable for you. It is helpful to have a coach on the sidelines who can observe the game and advise you from an objective standpoint. Now is the time to select a coach. Assume the role of the high diver again. To prepare for the world-championship dive it would seem logical to select a coach experienced in what you want to achieve. A coach who:

- Knows your potential and can recognise your talent.
- Encourages your talent to use your intuition.
- Knows other experts in the field that you can consult should you need to.
- Respects your right to express yourself and allows you to perform the world-championship dive as you wish to express it.

Let's look at the areas that may require attention. If we are going to dive into a pool, can we swim? Sounds basic doesn't it? Yet if we can't swim, we may make the first practice dive and never get to the real event. Is our physical fitness at a level that will enable us to make the dive? Will our muscles respond the way we want them to? Do we know what type of dive will score the most points? Remember, when we make the world-championship dive, others will score us. It will be others who will decide how well we performed. Other people will reflect our own judgements, beliefs and criticisms. Our coach must be able to assist us in all the above and bring other expertise when required. Our coach is a very special person who must have our confidence. The selection of our intuitive coach is vital.

There are many names for our intuitive coach. The new age talks about spirit guides. Christianity refers to guardian angels, and I am sure other groups have names for their coaches. My point is that we access and talk to our coach intuitively. Intuition is the language of the multi-dimensional world. It is here that the soul lives. It is this source that is our ultimate coach. As your intuition takes root in the spring time of its development, allow it to direct you to your intuitive coach. Spring time is the time to access your intuitive coach and speak with your soul.

Because we live in the linear dimension, we often feel more comfortable with tangible things. We have greater confidence in objects that we can touch, feel, smell, and hear than in the intangibles. Through experience we have learnt to trust our senses implicitly. We know, for example, that a fire is dangerous because we have experienced being burnt, seen another burnt, heard about burn victims on the news broadcasts and so on. In the spring time we need to experience our intuition in play so that we learn to trust it in the same way we trust our tangible senses. When we are confident with our intuition it will lead us to the soul. The soul shows itself in many forms and in many situations. When we listen to our intuition and observe our lives dispassionately we will find our coach. Our coach is in everything that has life in it. Developing confidence in our coach takes time. So play with your intuition patiently. In this part of spring time choose your coach to help you bring your intuition out into the fields to play.

THE USES OF ENTHUSIASM

Remember the farmer who was so keen for his crops to grow that he went out at night and tugged at the shoots? Enthusiasm and excitement are wonderful. They can generate amazing amounts of energy in our lives. The problem is that this kind of enthusiasm, by its very nature, is short-lived. All it does is to bring the hidden possibilities into view. Enthusiasm tempts us to rush out and do things before we formulate any sensible plans.

This happened to me while writing this book. Initially I wrote each chapter freehand but I quickly became frustrated with this method and began to think of alternatives. One day, after meditating, I felt that I should dictate the text. The idea was born and I was enthusiastic about it. Without further thought I set up the tape recorder and let fly with pearls of wisdom. It was great! The thoughts came and it was taking about a tenth of the time. Ironically, the subject was about enthusiasm.

I must have dictated for about thirty minutes then, as the energy began to wane, I looked down at the microphone and realised that I had not switched it on. Can you imagine how I felt? I had lost it all. I sat with feelings very different to my initial excitement. My first thought was that the dictation didn't work because the intuition was incorrect. Isn't it interesting how we try to justify our mistakes instead of looking for the positive lessons in them? Note the linear reaction. Note how I immediately chose to discount the information instead of looking for the lesson. Fortunately, I quickly realised that what I was trying to teach others I had just done myself!

The message was quite clear. If we begin any project out of enthusiasm alone, then we are very likely to lose the detail before we have fully integrated it. Once you have visualised, imagined and formalised your plan in the winter time, *do nothing about it — yet.*

Enthusiasm is important. It is like that big burst of energy that propels a rocket into space. It is the first stage of the rocket thrust. It is what will give us all the power to lift us off the ground. It is the energiser that pushes the intuitive shoot from the seed, through the soil and into the physical dimension. Enthusiasm is an emotion with a short life. When it arrives, it does so with immediate intensity. You will also find that it disappears at the same speed. Enthusiasm is the rocket booster. It is the initial thrust that breaks through our linear resistance and all of those beliefs that are holding us back. It is the thrust that is going to take you into another dimension. It is the thrust that is going to loosen the linear bonds.

Have you ever been to a sales conference where they spend a lot of time building enthusiasm? You know they are building it to sell you something you may not want or to tell you something you don't want to hear or motivate you to do something that you don't want to do. Selling happens in everyday life. Selling happens everywhere. Think about the people who have tried to persuade you to do something and how they use feelings of excitement to achieve their objectives.

Enthusiasm will move us off our current plane of reality and into new opportunities. Enthusiasm is important because it enables us to see things from a new perspective. However, if you think that enthusiasm is going to take you all the way then you have lost the plot.

An adrenalin rush may convince us that we can do anything. We are going to achieve our dreams. We can see it. We can feel it. It is wonderful! We rush out and start talking about it. By talking about it we begin to expend the energy of enthusiasm. The fuel of the rocket booster is being used up faster. Remember, the faster we use up the fuel of enthusiasm, the closer we will remain to the earth's surface. We need to integrate our enthusiasm within ourselves for maximum effect.

How do you imagine a sales force would react to their manager who excitedly presented an unprepared sales program to them? It is imperative to have our ideas completely integrated within us to inspire confidence in others.

So why do we rush out before it is time? Perhaps we are influenced by our egos and have gone out there to find reinforcement for an idea that may or may not be achievable. Now there are belief systems and there is knowing. We reach our full potential when we act from our knowing. Your belief system comes from your ego conditioned by linear thought. We all have beliefs. We all have attachments. We all have attitudes. They are our security in the linear perspective. When our egos function from linear beliefs, we need to be very, very careful how we express our enthusiasm.

The farmer in spring time doesn't know which seed will grow at the time of planting. This knowledge is within the seed. We need to allow the seed to develop away from the harsh external environment. It needs to send its roots down first, where no one can see it growing, before it starts to send the shoot to the surface. Enthusiasm and love fertilise the intuitive life force.

THREE PERSONALITY TYPES

When we take our intuition into the linear dimension we will meet three types of people. The first type are critical analysers. These people specialise in pulling ideas apart. Innovation and enthusiasm scare them. Critical analysers will say things like, 'Come on it really won't work. Have you considered that I know someone and she tried this and, um, there are fifteen million other people that are all trying to do this and it just won't work'. Critical analysers live in the linear dimension and feed off the destruction of ideas. They usually live in victim consciousness and have an encyclopedia of reasons why not to live at all. Because of their belief system, they are frightened to venture out and risk failure — a notion that is non-existent to the intuitive person.

If we are not strong in ourselves and if we haven't let go of our old beliefs, then these people will feed off us. That old part of us may also rise up again and say, 'Now hang on a minute, maybe they're right. Thanks, I really thought I had a good idea there' and we will walk away and let it go.

The second personality type is the friend who really wants to help you because he or she just loves giving advice. This category is potentially more dangerous than the first. Your friend will say things like, 'It is wonderful. It is great. You really ought to go ahead. This is fantastic. I really wish I had thought of the idea.' Then they will bring in that little word that says *but*. Watch out for 'but' words. Watch what is said after 'but'. These people are the white ants of society; they are going to say everything supportive to you and then stick in a 'but' to throw in the seeds of doubt.

Both these categories of people have one thing in common. They are telling you about your plans as if they were you. In reality, they are not you. If, when we associate with these people, we feel drained of energy it is because we are allowing them to puncture our fuel tank of enthusiasm. The person that is responsible for losing the fuel is you. Always remember that.

The third type of personality is the multi-dimensional personality or the intuitive. When we tell them our ideas, they will look at us with love and respect. Listen politely to us then get on with their lives and respect our right to do the same.

WORKSHOP *(allow one hour)*

This is the time to invigorate your intuition with the energy of life. It is the time to feed your intuition and to look at those areas of your life that are restricting the life flow. It is also the time to meet your coach; the total knowing of the soul.

Have you noticed that the workshops are getting smaller as we progress? You will find that the more you access your intuition the more your intuition will take over your lessons. We use the process of meditation to allow your intuition to manifest and balance. So, find a relaxed position and:

Breathe deeply and affirm as you breathe in:

I AM the infinite and intelligent life force

Exhale and relax more deeply than before. Breathe deeply and affirm as you breathe in:

I AM the infinite and intelligent life force

Exhale and relax more deeply than before. Breathe deeply and affirm as you breathe in:

I AM the infinite and intelligent life force

Exhale and relax more deeply than before. Breathe deeply and affirm as you breathe in:

I AM the infinite and intelligent life force

Exhale and relax more deeply than before.

Draw your attention to the base of your spine and feel an energising heat rising up through your body. As the sensation of warmth fills you, notice that the most vibrant red is now all around you and flooding into you. Travel along the red rays until you arrive in a classroom. There standing next to a huge whiteboard is a teacher with whom you instantly develop a very close rapport. This teacher is there to talk to you, advise you, instruct you and answer any questions that you wish to ask. This teacher may speak to you directly, write on the white-board or send the messages through your feelings. Spend the meditation time of thirty minutes in this classroom being ener-gised with the colour red and learn about your life force.

After the meditation record any thoughts that you wish in your work book. Realise that you are more intuitive, healthier and wealthier than before. Affirm that you are the infinite intel-ligent life force. Close the session by visualising a blue light wrapping you up from head to foot Then change the light to silver and then to gold.

SUMMARY

1   This is a time when we begin to experience glimpses of the new life that living intuitively creates.

2   Intuition can only be born and grow in love. Love is the multi-dimensional environment. By planting and growing your intuition in this dimension you give it total intelligence and possibility.

3   In spring time many opportunities, dreams of the future and new sensations emerge. The meaning of these new situations and thoughts can sometimes be misinterpreted.

4   At this point in our intuitive development when the life force is surging into consciousness, the ego will project all that is within our linear reality on to the screen of life.

5   The selection of our intuitive coach is vital and we need to do this before we enter the multi-dimensional universe.

6   Our spirit or eternal life force dwells in the multi-dimensional world, where the source of everything is and from which we can draw. It is this source that is our ultimate coach.

7   If we commence any project purely out of enthusiasm then we are very likely to lose the detail before we have fully integrated it into our consciousness.

8   Enthusiasm is an emotion; it is like that rocket booster that can break us loose, that can move us off our plane of current reality and take us to new dimensions.

9   There are beliefs and there is knowing. We always succeed when we come from our knowing.

SPRING

Practise, Practise, Practise

Transformation continues subtly. The sharp contrast between winter and spring fades from memory. As all growth is now subtle, so too is the transformation of spring to summer. Subtle hints are evident as temperatures creep upwards. Butterflies emerge from their infancy. Blossom falls to earth leaving the young fruits to continue their growth to maturity. Spring rains give way to winds of a different nature. The time of water is changing subtly to air.

Notice the subtlety of water as it moves across the earth. Notice the subtle changes the winds bring to the water. Notice the effect of the sun's fire on the waters of the planet.

All at this time is subtlety. Subtlety in transformation. The subtlety in stillness. The meaning of gentleness. This is a time to stay alert, refine your intuition and observe the subtleties within.

S PRING TIME IS nearly complete. Go out and find a patch of lush green grass underneath a shady tree and listen to the water running over the rocks of the nearby stream. See the butterflies dancing on the breeze. We reflect on the past. We dream into the future. We recognise that this time will soon be over and the time of summer will be upon us. Summer time is a time of seasonal extremes, a time of hot winds, rainstorms and long stretches of daylight and hard work. It is through the summer time experience that our intuition matures. We have cleared our barns, sharpened our tools, planted and watched the birth of our intuition.

Spring is an exciting time, full of activity, contrasts and rapid growth. We can see things happening because everything seems to grow so fast. Yet we know that as summer draws near there will be a lot of work with less obvious results, longer hours and greater effort. Naturally, the last month of spring is the perfect time to prepare for summer.

Many things will have changed in your life since you began reading this book. Your thoughts are beginning to have an effect on your external environment. The change in yourself appears as results in the linear world.

REVISION

Consider that the two realities, linear and multi-dimensional, are linked and operate for different yet compatible reasons. In the linear world, we look for evidence to help us evaluate our position and make the necessary changes for growth. Our personality functions in this realm. The multi-dimensional realm, on the other hand, has total creative possibility and therefore total creative thought. All thought is just sitting there. It is a cumulation of all our experiences and understanding that we have in the linear universe. This is the realm of our soul. It is the source of the divine creative energy of love. Our intuition moves between these two dimensions. It is able to link and integrate our beings. Our soul functions in the multi-dimensional reality. Our personality (physicalness) functions in the linear universe.

THE NEED MODEL

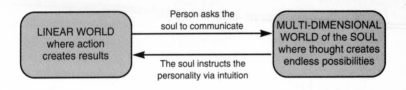

Do you remember this graphic? When our personality wants to create, it sends a request to the soul. The soul explores the multi-dimensional world and selects those thoughts that will manifest the required result in the physical, linear dimensions. Similarly when our soul seeks more experiences, it signals your personality to take more creative possibilities (thoughts) into the linear world and look for more experiences. Our ego is amoral. It respects the right and validity of thoughts either from the personality or the soul. It is the motivator. It is the vehicle that brings form to conscious intelligence in the linear world.

Our intuition is the knowing. It can recognise the difference between intelligent thought from the soul and beliefs of the personality in the linear world. Beliefs are simply interpretations without substance resulting from observations in the physical dimensions. Our intuition acts as the safety valve, the judge and the jury of our total functioning. It is the knowing. This is the process behind the idea that thought creates reality.

When the soul passes instructions to your personality, the ego doesn't judge the efficacy of the instruction. It merely responds to the request. Therefore it is important to know yourself because what you ask for you will get. When we work from linear reality, the signals can not be one hundred per cent of what we consciously want because they are coloured by our illusory beliefs. To develop intuitively, we must acquire the skill to go into the soul and choose correctly the thought that will create perfectly what we require.

THE CREATIVE POWER OF IMAGINATION

We have discussed at considerable length the two realities. Have you ever wondered where thoughts come from, what they are, and what or whom they represent? I want you to consider an idea now that, should you choose to accept it, will radically alter your life. It will so totally change your life that you need to think carefully before reading on. Sounds dramatic doesn't it? The fact is that our thoughts create and alter our reality — every thought. Therefore everything that we sense, in this case read, will manifest in some shape or form in our experiences.

To develop our intuition or any project at this stage we use the power of thought via our imagination. We think things into reality, therefore, whatever we imagine will at some time manifest in the physical world. To develop intuitively, we must use intuitive imagining and allow our intuition to instruct the ego to select the proper creative thoughts. Meditation can be used for creative visualising.

There is a fundamental difference between *Living Intuitively* and most other actualisation techniques. Instead of suggesting that you work out what it is you want, picture it, imagine it, feel it and affirm it (in other words use the linear approach of desire and sensation). I am suggesting that, in an open, non-desirous manner, you allow your intuition to instruct your soul to bring to you the most suitable and desired result for your development at the time you ask for it. Allow yourself to be the vehicle for universal creation instead of the dictator of desire.

This is a time to practise and refine, practise and refine, practise and refine. It is a time to imagine, dream, become excited and continually refine your thoughts about your project.

WORKSHOP (allow one hour)

This is the last phase of the spring of your intuitive development. There is nothing to do except practise the art of intuition. Practise it. Practise it. Practise it.

It is important now to select your practice ground so that you can practise without distraction. A good practice ground will be different for each person. Here are some guidelines that may be of use.

- A quiet environment where you are free from interruption.
- An environment that makes you feel totally safe.
- Wear comfortable clothes.
- Train yourself to practise at set times of the day.
- For variety, learn to use your imagination in many situations. Change your practice environment when you become bored with it.
- Allow nature to assist you. Walk along a beach, sit by a river, go to the mountains.
- Always carry a pen and paper with you to record your intuitive thoughts and the results of your practice sessions.

EXERCISE

This is the practice session. Do it often. In this meditation I want you to let your imagination go wild. Use the following points to stimulate your imagination. Don't force what comes into your mind. Send out the imagined thought and wait for your soul to send the picture back. Relax into your practice ground and prepare yourself for meditation.

1 Imagine the benefits of making more important decisions instantly.
2 Imagine having the ability to be innovative.
3 Imagine being able to make plans effortlessly.
4 Imagine being able to implement your plans successfully.
5 Imagine being able to do all of the above intuitively.
6 Imagine living intuitively.
7 Imagine yourself being able to find the answers inside yourself to resolve your problems.
8 Imagine your success.
9 Imagine your prosperity.
10 Imagine your intuitiveness.

Breathe deeply and affirm:

I AM the essence of creativity
I AM perfectly creative now.
I create only in the energy of perfect love

Breathe deeply and affirm:

I AM the essence of creativity
I AM perfectly creative now
I create only in the energy of perfect love

Breathe deeply and affirm:

I AM the essence of creativity
I AM perfectly creative now
I create only in the energy of perfect love

Breathe deeply and affirm:

I AM the essence of creativity
I AM perfectly creative now
I create only in the energy of perfect love

As you are relaxing, you become aware of an indigo light shining in the centre of your forehead. The indigo light floods into your body and surrounds you heightening your awareness. It takes you to a river that leads to endless possibilities. Relax in the stream and allow it to take your imagining wherever you wish it to go.

After thirty minutes finish the meditation and record anything that you wish to. End the session by wrapping yourself completely in the blue light that changes to silver and then gold.

SUMMARY

1   Prepare for summer time. In the next phase, you will experience a time of seasonal extremes, a time of hot winds, heavy rains, long stretches of daylight and work.

2   Our thoughts are the very central point of creation in the external environment. The evidence of creative thought, appears as results in the linear world yet we draw our thoughts from the multi-dimensional world.

3   The two universes are linked and operate for different yet compatible reasons. The linear world helps us to evaluate ourselves. The multi-dimensional universe has total creative possibility and therefore total creative thought.

4   Our intuition is the go-between of these two dimensions, being able to link and integrate our beings.

5   Our intuition is the 'knowing' and has the ability to recog-
    nise intelligent thought from the multi-dimensional world
    and distinguish it from the 'beliefs' of the personality in the
    linear world.

6   When developing as an intuitive person, we must acquire
    the skill to go into the multi-dimensional world and chose
    correctly the intelligence to create perfectly what we
    require.

7   To use our intuition we move inwards to the multi-dimen-
    sional universe, and then via ego we project outwards into
    the physical linear world.

10

A Time of Endurance

I looked at the wind and felt its confusion
I listened to the wind and saw its inconsistency
I felt the wind and heard its intensity
And I wondered

We walked through the summer time, my intuition and I
Sometimes together and sometimes apart, or so it seemed
My heart yearned for spring and beat silently lest my
intuition walk by.

Where has it gone to or is it still with me?
Intuition or illusion I cannot tell
Yet know it is there, somewhere.

To what end am I labouring in the heat that can drain?
Oh where are the results to show what I have gained?
My mind is weary yet my heart is strong

My dreaming is ceaseless yet reality lives on
Intuition I understood or so I thought
Was out there somewhere
Yet when I tell others they look at me strange
and talk of the wind and gaze away.

THE FARMER ROSE with the sun on the first day of summer. He walked outside and felt the difference. He had been through many summers before. At the start of each, the feeling was the same, although the outcomes were different. He knew there was much to do to provide the best conditions to produce the best crops. Desire, he thought, was an emotion that he would prefer to let go of in summer. With a growing sense of restlessness he dressed and went out to the barn to find comfort from the good memories of the past. When he got there, he remembered that the old machinery had gone. He had given those outmoded elements of his life away. The barn was empty apart from the necessary tools that were his workshop.

He knew that this season would seem longer than the rest. He would be out in the fields longer. He would need to work harder and would always be trying to anticipate changes in the weather in time to protect his crops. He wondered what challenges he would face this year and prayed silently for the strength, the power and the zeal to satisfactorily travel through the season of summer. There was little comfort in the barn that morning. The memories had gone. He knew that to try to find them would only distract him from his mission and purpose. If he wanted peace of mind then he knew it was through the satisfaction of applying his talents to the challenges to come.

THE ATTITUDE OF SUCCESS

The summer time in our intuitive development can be very challenging. It is characterised by:

- Rapid change in weather patterns (unpredictability).
- Huge variances in temperature (emotional swings).
- Unpredictable rains (deep-seated beliefs to release).
- Predators trying to eat the crops before they are ready for harvest (people wanting to live off your success).

This is the testing season. It will test us because we always have a choice. Our attitude is crucial to our success. We can view the challenges of the season in linear terms, and judge them to be pests and other undesirable elements or we can see them as perfect realities supporting our intuitive growth.

When I was a boy, I remember visiting my relatives on their

farm. At the weekend we attended the local church service. It had been a particularly testing time for the farmers. During the previous week, a plague of locusts had eaten almost everything in its path. The air was so thick with insects that we could not use a car because they would have clogged up the engine's cooling system. The locusts had eaten out many farms. So at this particular church service there was a feeling of sorrow and many people asking, 'why me?'

The minister, in an attempt to focus on the positive, asked the congregation if there was anything good that had happened the week before. After a short pause a person stood up and thanked God because, although the locusts had eaten out the surrounding properties, they did not touch his. As he sat down there was another shuffle at the back of the church. This time a little old man rose from his seat and faced the congregation.

'The locusts completely ate my crops', he said. 'There is nothing left to show for the season' and then tears came to his eyes as he said, 'I would just like to say that any time God wishes to graze his locusts on my land I would be honoured.' This man's face was radiating with peace and happiness. His eyes shone with an enthusiasm for life that has remained in my memory.

Your attitude and perspective is of the utmost importance. The attitude you take will reflect your thoughts in the world that you choose as your reality. I knew nothing of multidimensional realities back then. Yet I know that this little old man was a part of it.

THE SEASONS REVISITED

It seems that in summer all the elements unite in conflict, stir each other up, and interact with each other in many ways. The world becomes an amphitheatre in the summer. It can be a time of great confusion when the hopes of spring fade from our memories as the physical effort increases to support the growth of the crops. As the excitement of spring fades, change becomes more subtle yet at the same time intensifies. It is a season of dichotomy.

In the winter there was plenty of time to reflect, take things at an easy pace and look forward to results that we knew were attainable at some future point. Yes, the waiting was frustrating. So in winter we learnt to be patient. We learnt how to discipline the mind; how to concentrate on the present; release the past; and how to visualise the future. Winter was a time to formulate plans, search for ideas and adjust our environments. In the winter time we prepared ourselves for the world championships through active inactivity. Our intuition was yet to be born.

When spring arrived we celebrated the birth of our intuition and nurturing. It was a time of nurturing excitement. Spring time gave us great inner satisfaction and encouragement because now we could see the evidence of our inner knowing. With excitement it was easy to raise our energy levels. It was easy to dance to inspiring music. Everything was fresh and new. Our ideals seemed to be purer than pure. Nothing could go wrong in the spring time because our optimism was infectious. People around us witnessed the emergence of the new us. We experienced the energy of enthusiasm.

Remember, that we are treating the development of our intuition as a project, because once we have learnt how to develop this project then we can use our intuition to build project after project after project. Intuition is the basis of creativity and we can apply it to any of our endeavours.

It may seem contradictory but to access our intuition we must do it intuitively. This is the nature of working from the multi-dimensional perspective and it is in the summer time that we crystallise this idea. Concepts, ideas, ambitions, dreams and goals cannot be fully effective until we integrate them into our consciousness, which is us. Until our projects become us they won't realise their full potential. So summer is the time of integration; it is the time to internalise the externalities.

We function to a major extent in the linear universe. This is the universe of externality, the illusion of cause and effect, the use of outcomes to reinforce beliefs. In fact, what we see outside ourselves and sense all around provides the proof of our intuition at work. In the spring time our intuition literally bursts into our linear environment so that we can see it, evidence it, touch it, and believe it. Remember, belief is a part of the linear dimension. When we come from the linear perspective belief is imperative as a reinforcer, albeit temporary; it encourages us to search for the knowing. Spring time is the reinforcer.

THE STEELING PROCESS OF SUMMER

We are moving from the highly sensory condition of spring to the more subtle integrating season of summer. Summer can seem endless. We work on our plans unceasingly because we know we no longer have the luxury of time. This is a time that requires great inner strength to persist and mental commitment to the job at hand.

It is also a time of doubts and wondering. You wonder whether your planning and preparation was sufficient. You try to keep your objectives clearly in mind. There can be times during this part of a project where doubts surface about yourself. It is a time of self-evaluation.

Reflect on the farmer for a moment. During winter he assesses his machinery, his resources, looks at the past sales history of the markets, makes judgements about the future demand, looks at the production capability of his farm and the profitability of various comparative crops. He decides to plant wheat, barley and corn, based on his knowledge at the time.

What if the farmer begins to doubt his previous judgements? Maybe he should have grown flowers and diversified into sheep, run some cattle, a little for meat and some for milk. Imagine if he began to panic so much that he went to the bank and re-financed, bought a herd, installed milking sheds and so on. Imagine the consequences of starting over. It seems ridiculous doesn't it. Yet we do it so often in our lives. Maybe we have a fear of success; maybe it is the fear of failure or a lack of confidence, who knows Frequently, we become disillusioned in the middle of a project when obstacles come into our path, and we panic and change direction. When you drop a project you usually revert to the winter time of the seasonal cycle.

People who try very hard to change their recurring patterns usually get stuck at the summer time of their development. This season is critical. Change will not occur until your dreams become a part of you. We can foster brilliant ideas, put them out there and receive all the praise that is possible. But when we arrive at the summer time of the cycle we find ourselves alone in the field with only our talents and the task in front of us. The task of integration and internalisation has begun and it is the summer time that is the pivot of change. In summer we should stamp the words of Sir Winston Churchill everywhere that we can read them.

Never give in. Never give in. Never give in.

This is the season when you can change your patterns; realise your goals; discover your unique talents; and become intuitive.

SUMMARY

1   The summer time of our intuitive development can be challenging. Just as the season of summer is noted by extremes, fast weather changes, huge variances in temperature, unpredictable rains and the arrival of predators who wish to live off the crops before they are ready for harvest, so it is with our intuitive development.

2   Your attitude and perspective will be reflected in the world that we choose to be our reality.

3   As there is permanence in the seasons when viewed from the perspective of the soul, so too is there permanence in the technique of developing intuition that can be applied to any of our endeavours.

4   Summer is the time of integration. It is the time to internalise the externalities.

5   People who have recurring patterns in their lives are usually stuck at the summer time of their development.

6   Summer is the time to change your patterns; realise your goals; discover your unique talents; and become intuitive.

11

Be Excited by the Experience

The sun reaches for its zenith, growth continues. The farmer tends the crops, always watchful, supportive, always encouraging the growth of the potential within and protecting the plant from any influence that will restrict its growth.

The days are long, the season hot. In toil, strength comes and stamina increases.

While the fool curses the sun, the length of the days and the intensity of effort, the sage learns his lessons by unconditional giving.

Keep your sense of purpose, be assured in its direction and experience your world.

Notice the wind shifts, feel refreshed by the rains and grow straight, strong and upwards.

THINK BACK TO a successful project. Can you remember your initial feeling of elation when the first wins came through? Can you remember how quickly the excitement died down? The zing of success in the linear world doesn't last long. Indeed, it seems that the more we become used to something, in this case success, the less we feel excited about it.

Relationships can be like this. At first when we fall in love everything is vibrant. Everything is perfect. People say that we see everything through rose-coloured glasses. I have heard these magical spectacles described as devices that cover up reality, because through them everything looks perfect. In the linear world, perfection may not be obtainable. Perfection is out there somewhere. We search for it. We strive for it. We even chase after it. Yet somehow when we reach it, we can only hold on to it for a short time. Perfection somehow leaps away from us again and the chase continues.

THE ILLUSION OF DEFICIT NEED

We feel fulfilled when we strive for perfection. Ambitious people forever talk about the effort they put into their achievements. Psychologists talk about needy dependent personalities; people who feel worthwhile only when they are striving to satisfy a particular need. This need we define as a deficit that requires filling. When we are in deficit we are in debt. We owe someone something. Within this needy dependent state there are conditions upon conditions upon conditions and with it assumptions upon assumptions upon assumptions. Some successful sales people will tell you that they work the hardest and most productive when they are striving to attain something that they don't have.

Offering people things to fill up their need tanks can be an ideal perfect motivator. For example, if you were a sailing enthusiast without a yacht, then I could motivate you by offering you one as an incentive to work harder, longer and to make sacrifices to earn it. In life, the reward systems are many. They are intrinsic to the linear world. Incentives use the belief of deficit need.

So what happens when a person satisfies the need? What happens to the person when he or she achieves the goal and satisfies the need? The needy personality believes that self-worth directly relates to need satisfaction. Logically then the individual becomes, on achieving the goal, worthless. It is an interesting dilemma isn't it? What do we do when we satisfy the need?

The options seem to be:

1 We can accept our achievement and be excited by it (fulfilment).

2 We can create harder-to-achieve goals and place ourselves in a situation of greater need again (need creation).

3 We can anticipate the satisfaction of the need, panic, and sabotage the project before we achieve the goal (need stagnation).

Options 2 and 3 place you happily back into deficit need again. Look around you. You will see many people forever creating needs. They act out the same old patterns because they believe they are unable to change the cycle. They have chosen for themselves their very own deficit need–satisfaction principle. In the linear sense, perfection and fulfilment are out there as goals to strive for. What we meet along the way are hurdles to overcome to reach this nirvana! These rose-coloured glasses give us a glimpse of perfection which linear thought defines as unattainable. What happens, then, if what we see through the rose-coloured glasses is reality and all else is illusion? Have you thought of that?

EXPECTATION IS A CRUTCH

Reconsider the romantic situation. The infatuated state, just like any initial burst of excitement, doesn't last for long. When lovers first meet they have no expectations of each other. They fall in love innocently. Their excitement level is so high it suppresses past beliefs. The same happens with the birth of a child or an idea; we ride along on the cosmic adrenalin wave of excitement. Nothing else matters. For a time the world as we see it is perfect. Remember that I am talking here about the linear dimension. As the excitement ebbs, the energy levels drop and we rebalance again. At this time our belief system, patterns and conditioning re-emerge and the rose-coloured glasses dim. Before long doubts creep in. Expectations about how the other person should act become more important than experiencing the innocence. Eventually, we begin to suspect that the person is not who we thought she or he was. We feel disillusioned, hurt and the momentum of the relationship slows.

Once when I was going through some difficult moments I sought out a friend for advice. I felt sorry for myself and tried to solicit his support. I wanted him to agree with me and fully expected it. The issue was concerning another friend who I felt had let me down. Fortunately though, I have wonderful friends who know how to pass on advice, gently. Here I was talking to my friend Paul, feeling sorry for myself, when he stopped me and said, 'Bruce you are responsible for your life'.

'Yes,' I said, 'I know that'.

'Then how can people let you down?', he continued, 'unless you were leaning on them first.'

His response stopped me in my tracks. He was right! What right did I have to lean on a person at all?

When we create an expectation to lean on, ultimately we will experience disappointment if we are let down. Unless we take responsibility at the outset for our intuitions we stand the strong chance of relying on their expected outcomes. Expectations are projections about the future. Intuition lives in the present. The two never meet at the same time. When an idea develops and a project is born, the love affair happens in the spring time. It is the same with our intuition. In spring we see it for what it is and fall in love with it without any expectations. When we move into summer, the energy changes from one of excitement to one of familiarity. Be wary about expectations creeping in. They will take away the aura of freshness. In other words, summer is the time to move into the dimension of the soul. It is here that expectations are absent. Here, everything is and that is all there is to it.

There is a need to be strong as summer commences. We need to develop the strength of mind that will steel the will to go into our inner quietness and strengthen our resolve. To develop intuition beyond the spring time we must persist with it.

The notions about perfection and intuition are the same. Perfection is not out there somewhere. Perfection is here now. Perfection is the present moment. It is the soul. Again we can see how the differences in our understanding of linear states and soul affect our ability to produce results. In linear terms, perfection lives outside the present moment because it is out there in the future. Perfection in soul terms is here right now. You are perfect right now. I am perfect right now. We are perfect right now.

THE PREDICTIVE CRUTCH

Linear thought lives in the past or the future because it exists outside the present moment. Intuitive thought lives in the present moment. People living in the present moment live intuitively. People who live outside the present, that is in either the past or the future, think that the now is somewhere out there. They never find it. People who live in the linear world will use intuition to evaluate the past or predict the future. It is helpful to anticipate projected results. Yet, if we rely on the predictions without working towards them, then they have no value right now.

The creative person will use his or her intuition in the universe of the soul to create infinite opportunity, accept infinite reward and know that she or he is prosperous now. Summer is the time of continual decision-making in each moment. There will be choices about whether to revert to the patterns of the linear world or whether to move into the multi-dimensional reality. This is a moment by moment choice. This is a choice that you will make each time your energy level drops. Making this choice will forge strength in your intuition.

In summer your intuition will become powerful, energetic, vital and free. You intuitions will become more real to you and will help you to increase your expertise across as many facets of your life that you choose. Above all your intuition will come of age in the summer time. It will change your outlook on life to a now look on life. As our projects begin to yield fruit we will observe our intuition becoming stronger within us. It is becoming a part of us, so that our belief in the intuitive process transforms into the knowing that our intuition *is* us. We will have developed a steadfast belief that all experiences are good. We will have developed a persistence in expecting this good. We will be able to withstand the negative beliefs of the linear world and we will refuse to settle for less than the best in our life's experiences. It is by developing our intuitive strength that our intuition takes on substance.

WORKSHOP *(allow one hour)*

By now you may have noticed that we are using different colours in our meditations. Colours and music have specific vibrations that enhance the intuitive state. With each of the meditations in this book it is important to meditate using the colours specified. So here we go again. Find that perfect place for you and relax.

Breathe in deeply and relax as you exhale affirming:

I AM perfect strength now
My strength grows in love

And relax some more. Breathe in deeply and relax as you exhale affirming:

I AM perfect strength now
My strength grows in love

And relax some more. Breathe in deeply and relax as you exhale affirming:

I AM perfect strength now
My strength grows in love

And relax some more. Breathe in deeply and relax as you exhale affirming:

I AM perfect strength now
My strength grows in love

And relax some more.

Bring your attention to the small of your back. This is the place where you muster your strength from. Visualise shafts of red and yellow light flowing into this area and filling your body. The light and the colour are energising you now and it begins to flow out through the point between your eyebrows. Visualise yourself leaving your physical body and travelling along the rays of red and yellow and see where they take you.

Meditate on strength and your intuitive purpose for thirty minutes. Visualise the blue light encircling you after you have finished the meditation. Know that you are healthier, stronger and more intuitive than before. Take some time to record your experiences before you lose them.

SUMMARY

1   The summer time is the time to move into the dimension of the soul. It is here that expectations are absent. Here, everything is and that is all there is to it.

2   As summer commences, there is a need for strength so that we can travel into the quietness, to access more energy.

3   Perfection is the state of the present moment and, because of this, it is a part of the soul.

4   People who live in the linear world will use intuition to evaluate the past or predict the future; the intuitive person will use his or her intuition to create infinite opportunity, accept infinite reward and know that she or he is prosperous now.

5   The summer time is the time of continual decisions and choices. We make choices about whether to revert to the patterns and beliefs of the linear world or to move into the soul state of the now.

6   It is by using the strength that is within us and around us that our approach will change from the linear to the multi-dimensional.

12

Perfecting Your Style

Initial successes are exciting. They provide the adrenalin rush, and add to the excitement and euphoria of the realisation of your dream. Now is the time for radical choice. You can choose to live off this success or to increase your efforts and magnify the gains. The summer time is:

A time for weeding out.

A time for steadiness.

A time for consistent work.

A time for tireless effort.

A time of endurance.

A time of storms.

A time of continuing growth.

A time of ripening.

A time to experience the hot winds.

A time to understand your environment.

THE INTUITIVE CHOICE

By now you will be using your intuition and sensing its power. It's fun to demonstrate your newly found ability to those who haven't developed this aspect of themselves. To watch their surprise. Listen to their amazement and accept their praise. Intuitive people are always popular in groups. We can be very entertaining at dinner parties and other social gatherings. Try it out if you wish and watch how people react to you. I call using intuition in this manner 'party tricks'. It can be a lot of fun without much purpose. You will find that your popularity will rise.

Be aware that as your intuitive power grows so will your profile among others. People will want to benefit from your intuitive insights. Draw upon it. Use it and benefit from it. They will see something in you of value to themselves. They will want to use your intuition without going through the process of developing it for themselves. They will want what you have and will take it from you if you let them.

At the beginning of summer the fruit has set. The crops are showing their potential and farmers have choices to make. When will they harvest? What will they do with the harvest? How will they use the benefits that will come from their efforts? Now in our intuitive development we have the same choices to make. We can recognise our intuition and continue to develop it. We can use it to become popular. We can use it to produce results in the linear dimension. We can work with it, strengthen it and become more powerful with it. We can choose to acknowledge the responsibilities that come with a developed intuitive awareness. You will find that the new responsibilities will relate to your overall development at the time.

We have discussed the requirements for developing your intuition. The reality that you plant the intuitive seed into will determine its character. If you plant it in the linear soil then the results will be transitory. Should your ego manifest itself and you use your intuition to exploit people who are not as aware as you, then remember that you are functioning in the linear world. The consequences that result from your ego-driven desires will certainly enter into your experience.

Beware of individuals who rely on your judgement instead of using their own. They will effectively drain you of energy, no matter how altruistic you are. Here is an experience to illustrate the point.

In the role of a psychic I meet many people with varied backgrounds looking for answers. Sometimes after a reading I receive more information for them. On one occasion, I intuitively felt that I should contact a colleague. It seemed strange because it was several months since I gave her a reading. I kept pushing the urge away but eventually I picked up the phone and rang her. Fortunately, because Jacqui worked with her intuition, she was not surprised when I said,

'I don't know why I am ringing. Do you want to talk to me?'

Talk she did. She excitedly told me that she had just booked a holiday to Asia. Now, the next part of the story is often how intuition works because you feel bits at a time. As soon as she told me where she was going I knew intuitively that the reason for my call was to tell her that it was not safe for her to travel there.

That is what I did. I said that although I couldn't tell her why, I felt that she should change her plans. I gave her the message and the rest was up to her. Jacqui is a highly intuitive person. She sensed the truth of the message and said that she would change her plans. We said farewell and hung up.

The story doesn't finish here. Several days later she tracked me down and in a roundabout way gave me three possible destinations.

'Could I advise her which one to take?', she asked.

When people rely on your intuitive advice, it is natural to feel flattered. The temptation can be strong to plan other people's lives even when there is no intuitive basis for it. This particular time I had no more intuitive insight and told her so. You see Jacqui needed the first message. The rest was her choice. It was not for anyone else to interfere. If you allow people to depend on your intuition, I guarantee that your days (and nights) will become congested with people wanting you to do it for them. In effect, what you are doing is denying them their right to make choices and have experiences.

By the way, the reason that the message was given to Jacqui, we discovered later, was because the hotel where she had planned to stay was at the centre of a terrorist attack at the time she would have been there.

INTUITIVE ETHICS

I ask you to consider four points.

1   Your intuition is for your benefit, growth and prosperity.
2   Should you wish to use it for others then do so when your intuition urges you to do so, not when others ask you to perform.
3   Do not force your intuitive insight on another person or try to convince them that your intuition is right.
4   Respect a person's right of choice.

SUBTLE WEEDING

Now that our intuition is more obvious we will also be able to see the weeds we missed in the winter time. This is true of any project. When we are in the early developmental phases of a project, we clear out all the obvious attitudes and beliefs that we think will hinder the project. It is possible that we missed the hidden ones. When success comes our way we relax more. Let down our guard. The difference between winter and summer is that the weeds' roots will have grown among the roots of our intuitive plants. We need to loosen these intruders, skilfully, without disturbing the growing process.

When we find more weeds it helps to view this as a time of adjustment rather than a time of eradication. It may be that the damage caused by eradication is far worse than the benefits of clearing. It may be that for the duration of the season we may have to learn to co-exist with the problem. The positive aspect of this process is that more, subtle refinements will occur within to help us cope with the problems. The big lesson here is about tolerance. We often discover more about ourselves in times of apparent unpleasantness than in times of bliss.

Summer is particularly a time to learn how, when and in what quantities to use our intuition. Too much power can sometimes be damaging. Radical decisions can be quite costly. When the weeds appear in your projects, treat them gently with firm, consistent intuitive will. Remember when you start to develop your intuition the comparison between the ego projections and intuition is great. The more in tune we become, the more subtle is our development and hence the comparative edge diminishes.

Summer storms will appear exaggerated because the comparative benefits have diminished. Note that this is only a matter of perception. This phase of your intuitive development will test your mettle. It is an opportunity to experience your intuition, use it and witness the results. This is a time when you are drawing on the intuitive resource of the soul to create results in the linear world. This is what lasting creation is about. This is a time when you will discover talents that lay hidden beneath layers of conditioning.

Your intuition does not recognise conditioning. How can it? It lives in the world of total possibility. Therefore, as your intuition becomes stronger and more powerful, it will push through the layers of linear conditioning, breaking them up and pushing them away. Always remind yourself that storms are only indicators of positive change and rebalance.

WORKSHOP (allow one hour)

During the summer we are testing our power, internalising and strengthening our intuitive style. This is the season for perfection. This is the season to perfect our style.

EXERCISE

Resume your comfortable meditative position. Breathe in deeply and relax as you exhale affirming:

My intuition is perfectly powerful now
My intuitive power grows in love

And relax some more. Breathe in deeply and relax as you exhale affirming:

My intuition is perfectly powerful now
My intuitive power grows in love

And relax some more. Breathe in deeply and relax as you exhale affirming:

My intuition is perfectly powerful now
My intuitive power grows in love

And relax some more. Breathe in deeply and relax as you exhale affirming:

My intuition is perfectly powerful now
My intuitive power grows in love

And relax some more.

Focus your attention on the sensation of your breath as it travels across the back of your throat. Focus your awareness there. Visualise the colour blue moving into your body through this spot. It relaxes and energises you. Now, feel the power within you as the colour blue expands your intuitive awareness. Stay with this feeling for thirty minutes.

When your meditation ends, wrap yourself up in green light. Note that you are healthier, more energised and more intuitive than before.

Record the events of your meditation in your work book.

FIELDWORK (time allowed: unlimited)

Use your intuition in your everyday life and observe the outcomes. During this phase of your development, analyse and assess your intuitive style to consolidate it. In other words, practise integrating your intuition.

SUMMARY

1   Be aware that as your intuitive power grows so too will your profile among others.

2   As your intuition becomes more obvious you will be able to see if there are any weeds left over from the winter time; now is the time when they will become obvious. This is true of any project.

3   The summer time, in particular, is a time to understand our intuitive power and to learn how, when and in what quantities to use it.

4   Our intuition does not recognise conditioning. It lives in the world of total possibility.

5   During the summer we are testing our power, internalising and strengthening our intuitive style. This is the season for perfection. This is the season to perfect our style.

6   Summer is the time to use your intuition judiciously.

13

After Perfection —
What Then?

*The harvest has arrived! Now is the time to reap its benefits.
Take time to feel satisfied as you gaze over the shimmering
crops that offer you the reward for all your efforts.*

*Know that the harvest is right for you. Know that its
produce will feed the soul for future growth. Know that God
looks upon these crops with pleasure. This is a time to store
the harvest and reflect on the benefits of the season.*

*The fool gazes over the fields abundant with nourishment,
relaxes contentedly and forgets all time.*

*The sage remembers the storehouse patiently waiting to
receive its reward, and feels the urgency to harvest before
the winds of autumn arrive.*

IMAGINE THAT YOU are standing beside the diving pool. You look up because there is wild cheering and applause. The noise is so loud and the energy is so high! Goosebumps rise up all over your skin when you realise that all this excitement is for you. You did it! You made your final dive and it was perfect! The result that you dreamt about, planned for and practised for is now a reality. Standing perfectly still with the water dripping off you, you can take time to feel satisfied, proud and all the other emotions associated with this sense of achievement.

Photographers mass around you. Reporters want to know who you are and talk to you. You are famous. The dive was successful. Your intuition has come of age. The celebrations run well into the night and eventually you go to bed, rest and dream of the most powerful moment of your life to date. This mood continues for several days. Enthusiasm is high. There is lots to do. Then, one day, you decide you want to relive the moment. You go back to the pool. It is very different now. Although the weather is good, the water clear, and the pool still as inviting as ever, you become aware of the silence. Now standing beside the diving tower you look around and no one is there. They have all left and gone about their own lives. You have become to them a happy memory. A sense of regret creeps in when you realise that the moment is over. Standing there in the silence, you ask yourself — what now?

Each phase of a cycle has its own characteristics. Each part of a progression is part of what went before. Yet when one phase or step is over, the next is always new and unexplored, and you need to consider your choices afresh. We now have vibrant memories to fill our barns. Exciting times to reflect on and yes, we know we were successful.

CAN YOU TEACH AN OLD DOG NEW TRICKS?

Life is full of one-day wonders. In the volatile world of fame we see movie stars, sports people, and politicians quickly rise to notoriety and disappear at the same speed. In contrast, we see others who keep succeeding for many years. In any project, we have stages to go through and goals to achieve along the way. After each success we have choices to make about whether to build on them or not. The difference between the one-day wonder and the long-term success is that the latter has the drive, the desire and the attitude to capitalise on each step of the journey. This is the attribute of zeal.

At the end of the summer time you have developed and used your intuition in many ways with stunning success. I know this to be a fact. Your struggle, effort and toil is now bearing fruit. In your resting moments, thoughts about how you can improve on your achievements will come into your consciousness. Also, the temptation to rely on memories of past successes will be strong.

For example, when the personal computer first came on the Australian market everyone wanted one. Every business saw these machines as a way to grow sales, record information, allocate costs and make profits.In those days it was easy for computer salespeople to make impressive sales and earn large incomes from it. It was an industry where almost everyone succeeded. Years later, when the industry stabilised, sales became harder to win. I remember managing a sales team of six people then. They were all over thirty years of age and had successful careers. The prospect of managing them excited me. I thought I could sit back, relax a little, and watch the sales come in. Yet the end of month sales never came close to the projections given at the start of the month. Every time I asked either a salesperson or the sales group at a sales meeting why the sales were so low they would talk about their previous successes. To any plan that was presented to them, they would tell me how they had done it in the past. I could not get these experts to focus on our present situation. They were living in the past.

These salespeople did not want to recognise that the market had changed. Instead of building on their skills, they expected their past glory to succeed for them now. They were not willing to build on the experiences of their successes. Naturally, in time, each one left the company, not in particularly happy circumstances. I kept in contact with most of them and they are all making excellent sales now. Each one will tell you the same reason for their present success. When they were relying on the successes of the past, they were not selling. However when they used what they had learnt from that era in a positive way, they became more successful than before!

As you begin to experience the successes created by your intuition and how people now relate to you, be aware of the temptation to stop and settle for what you have grown to now, before you have internalised it. The farmer can look at his crop with pride but unless he harvests the crop, it will waste away. It is the same with intuition. We can look at it for as long as we choose but it is not until we start to harvest and use it that it will be of benefit to us.

We have discussed many things in this book so far. Hopefully you are doing the exercises, meditating and using your intuitive abilities. The integration process is almost complete for you. The internalisation of the intuitive technique will soon complete itself in time for the start of autumn. At the end of the summer experience, it is good to relax, view all that has gone before and accept with pride your achievements.

ZEAL — THE ART OF OPTIMISM

What is zeal? You could describe it as continuous optimism. A person becomes optimistic then enthusiastic and then what? We have spoken of the necessity to summon great strength to develop intuitive power. Now you need to summon your zeal. Zeal is sustained excitement. Zeal is not something that we can fake. It is a part of the soul. Anything short-lived and unsustained comes from the linear dimension. Permanence, as we have said previously, is a part of the soul. Zeal is an internal quality that is you. It is the very essence of the life force that underpins all growth and all enthusiasm. It is through your zeal that stamina emerges. Stamina is something that we learn. We generate it by moving in and out of the two dimensions. Stamina is a quality of great power.

We talk of projects. We talk of developing our intuition. The underlying philosophy or technology is the same. There are many intrinsic qualities necessary to achieve success in the linear world. They all live in the soul. We can freely move between these states according to what we want to achieve. The way to permanent change is to develop our intuition first, and it is when we near the autumn time that the most radical change will occur. This is the season where we change from the linear personality to the creative soul force. It is in the autumn time that your consciousness shifts realities from the linear to one of total, all-encompassing possibility.

FLEXIBILITY — A SOUL QUALITY

At the end of summer, learn the great power of flexibility as you use your intuition. Flexibility is a part of the soul because it is the attribute that covers all possibilities. Beliefs and belief systems are linear and prevent the individual from becoming flexible. If you follow this course intentionally, you will harvest the qualities born from your intuitive development. Internalise them and be one with them. When this occurs you will be able to draw the wisdom of the soul into the linear dimension. This will provide infinite, unstoppable growth and opportunity in your life. You will be able to act wisely, with dignity and sincerity as you expand your level of prosperity.

The intuitive person is one who draws upon this universal wisdom and relates it to the pragmatic real-life issues of the linear world. Your intuition is unique and is expressed through your total experience. Your personal characteristics enable you to absorb it as a part of your personality. Therefore in the linear dimension, intuition is different for each different personality. This is so and necessary. It is wise to accept all forms of intuitive expression from others, criticising no one.

COMPARATIVE DISADVANTAGE

Your intuitive insights are yours and exist for your benefit. Another's intuitive insights are for them. Comparison is invalid and will, ultimately, place you in the linear world again. When you work in an environment with intuitive people, it is productive to work with each other on the intuitive levels. Do this separately over a specific project and compare notes. The common points you find will be the base of the matter and will represent the building blocks on which to grow. The divergent viewpoints may identify specific talents that each intuitive has and may still be incorported to benefit the project. You may also find beliefs that inhibit the growth of the project. Once these beliefs are identified you can release them.

Be flexible with your intuition and be gracious to others who haven't yet developed it. Understand that they do not have the same insights as you.

As you reach the end of the summer time of your intuitive development, you need to be zealous in your use of intuition.

Apply it and use it for your benefit. It is yours now. If you choose to view it from a distance it will wither on the vine. Use it, use it and use it and it will increase and increase and increase.

WORKSHOP *(allow one hour)*

Resume your meditative stance (sounds like martial arts doesn't it?). Breathe in deeply and relax as you exhale affirming:

My intuition is infinitely creative and powerful now
I AM PROSPEROUS NOW

Breathe in deeply and relax as you exhale affirming:

My intuition is infinitely creative and powerful now
I AM PROSPEROUS NOW

Breathe in deeply and relax as you exhale affirming:

My intuition is infinitely creative and powerful now
I AM PROSPEROUS NOW

Breathe in deeply and relax as you exhale affirming:

My intuition is infinitely creative and powerful now
I AM PROSPEROUS NOW

Now focus your attention on the base of your skull. See the colours, blue and indigo, encircling your body and spinning faster and faster. You feel yourself travelling faster and faster. In a flash you move into hyper-speed and everything stops still. As you look around, you realise that you have moved into the multi-dimensional world of total opportunity.

Travel around this world for as long as you wish. Speaking to anyone you find. Feel the energy of the soul and listen to its infinite wisdom. After the meditation encase yourself in a white light that diffuses into the colours of the rainbow; red, orange, yellow, green, blue, indigo and violet.

You are healthier, happier, more prosperous and more intuitive than you were before. You are perfect where you are and who you are, and your prosperity is assured.

SUMMARY

1   Each phase of a cycle has its own characteristics; each part of a progression is part of what went before, yet when one

phase or step is over; the next is new and unexplored, and you need to consider your choices afresh.

2 The difference between the one-day wonder and the long-term success is that the latter has the drive, the desire and the attitude to capitalise on each step of the journey.

3 As you begin to experience the success created by your intuition and how people now relate to you, be aware of the temptation to stop and settle for what you have grown to now, before you have internalised it.

4 At the end of the summer experience, it is good to relax, view all that has gone before and accept, with pride, your achievements.

5 Zeal is continuous optimism.

6 Anticipate the autumn time when your consciousness will shift dimension from the linear to one of total, all-encompassing possibility.

7 The intuitive person is one who draws upon the universal wisdom of the soul and relates it to the pragmatic real-life issues of the linear world.

8 When your intuition is internalised you will be able to draw the wisdom of the soul into the linear dimension.

14

A Time to Reap Rewards

All was still, all was silent
The colours were vibrant
And while I watched
They fell majestically

The birds sought refuge amongst the leaves
Yet the leaves bade farewell to the trees, and fell
In the stillness the leaves fell silently
As though the trees were weeping

I could not understand it, yet I knew
I felt the sadness, the agitation, the mourning
And the birds kept searching
For the refuge that had departed

The forest was changing
Releasing the old with celebration
And bearing its bark and grandeur
Unashamed, defiant almost

I felt the wisdom and I understood
I had lost my belief, yet somehow I knew
The change had arrived, the seasons released
And I accept it now

My intuition stands tall in all its glory
The path that I travelled is evident to all
The scars of my past that I was afraid to see
Are here in their glory with my intuition and me.

IT HAS BEEN quite a journey searching for, discovering and using our intuition. When I began to write *Living Intuitively* I had an inkling, a vision, a knowing, many expectations and I will say now that the contents intuited in this book were sometimes as new to me as they may be for you. As I wrote, my thoughts were gradually overtaken with images, and with the images came fewer words. For quite some time this distressed me because I felt the need for words. Words are linear. They have meaning, definition and judgement attached to them. They build a frame of reference which allows us to communicate with others in the linear dimension. The soul is non-restrictive. It has no need for containment. It therefore speaks a language where words are not necessary. In the linear world you learn how to do things by establishing a logical premise and then building constructs upon it. In the multi-dimensional world the soul teaches by motivating your personality into action through a sense of knowing. Sometimes intuition speaks to us visually; sometimes through feelings — and always with knowing. Our linear mind needs words to hang its security on. We also need words to describe the soul's language in the linear framework. The intuitive person listens to the soul through their feelings. She/he puts this knowing into words.

The autumn time is perhaps the most majestic season of all. It is complete in its celebration. From the blaze of glory to the honest starkness of the trees. In the autumn time of your intuitive development you have the most meaningful choice of all to make. The question is whether you wish to be one with your soul or remain permanently in the linear realm. The choice is yours and yours alone. Autumn time is a time of completion. It can mean mourning for some and contentment for others depending on which universe you dwell in. You have experienced your intuition and you are ready to take the next step by allowing the limitations of the linear dimension to fall away from you. You can acknowledge intuitively the perfect creator that you are if you choose.

This is the big one because it requires faith to develop intuition and trust in the multi-dimensional universe. Ponder a while in the autumn and look for the evidences of intuition in your life — in you! This is the time when you begin to realise fully the benefits of your efforts. This is the time of transition from one reality to another. When you allow yourself to live intuitively, your inner self becomes obvious to the world. This transparent state can certainly take some adjusting to.

It takes courage to be intuitive because living intuitively requires you to live now and nowhere else. The imagery that is ever present in the autumn time leaves us without confusion. If we face the challenges of life squarely, its messages are direct. This is the time to be yourself without apology. This is the time to live as who you are without trying to manipulate events or other people to give you what you want.

Relying on outcomes keeps us away from the wealth that is ours to take now. When we focus on outcomes we project our thoughts, and therefore our intent, into the future. Living intuitively means that we live now for what today wants to give us. It is so easy to alter, slightly, our stance on a subject because we want the approval of someone, or when we know that we can get something by doing this. To use your intuition to its maximum potential you will need to be able to express yourself to the world directly. The autumn time is a time to learn about frank expression. It is a time when people will give us what we ask for because we asked for it. If in the autumn time your life is not working the way you want, look at the way you are expressing yourself. Any hints of manipulation will be obvious to others. Think of the trees when they lose their leaves. They can hide nothing. It is the same with us in the autumn time.

We have almost travelled the full seasonal cycle. We have worked very hard at times to bring all of those personality traits that are inhibiting us to the surface because it helps us to see our actions more clearly. But it also means that others can see us for who we are. It is human nature to want acceptance and respect. We love praise yet honest comment from our peers often unsettles us. We may not perceive these comments as helpful because, deep down, our ego wants to hear the glamour and tinsel of the linear world. For example, when a project is completed we enjoy being in a staff meeting to receive an award for the effort that we put in. This is the linear world and is important. Make no mistake about it. The soul on the other hand says, 'Let's evaluate all facets of our experiences to date so that we can learn from them, develop and grow some more'. The linear person views this reaction as potentially dangerous criticism. The soulful person will approach the task of evaluation with humility and honour the process.

Can you think of any really impressive photographs of trees; trees that have soul? The photos are usually in black and white or grey shades. The trees are usually old, gnarled, twisted and sometimes dying. We look at these pictures and feel the wisdom in the honesty of the tree. It stands there unashamed simply saying, 'This is who I am'. Photographers don't seem to have the same attitude to the sapling that is yet to experience life. Life's experiences, whether we perceive them as good or bad, contain the wisdom of the ages. No matter what we have done we should not try to hide nor apologise for it. Every action and deed is our experiential basis for growth and needs to be honoured as such.

It takes courage to stand before others in this manner. Standing without excuse, reason or rationale, simply saying we are who we are. It takes considerable practice to do this also. This is the role of the autumn. This is where we require our focus and effort. Practising what you believe in requires you to be strong and courageous. So just *let the change happen*. Convert your belief into knowing and remember that belief is thinking about it; knowing is doing it.

In this phase of your development you will learn how to relate to people differently. To work intuitively is egoless. There is no need for external praise. In autumn, feel the power of silence. The remaining workshop will take you from the linear to the soul should you so choose.

To develop the ability to be who you are in the world you need to be able to face your greatest critic. That critic is you. If you don't believe me then stand in front of a full length mirror naked. Do nothing except look at yourself without forming an opinion of who you are or what you should change about yourself. Just stand there and love what you see. A friend once went to a weekend seminar where about one hundred participants were required to do the entire course naked. After the weekend I spoke to my friend about it. She said that, to her surprise, she was not self-conscious about her nudity at all. After all everyone else was the same. She felt very good about this until the course presenter came up to her and asked her why she was hiding. 'I am not', she said. 'Oh, yes you are!', came the reply. 'Go and look at yourself in the mirror and tell me what you see', were her instructions. My friend followed the instructions and stood in front of the mirror looking at her naked body and wondered what the instructor was talking about. Then it hit her like a steam train. She realised that she was still wearing makeup. She told me that her first reaction was not to go back to the seminar if she had to take the makeup off. She did go back and learnt a valuable lesson about the masks that we wear. We all have masks. The more obvious ones you will have shed in previous seasons. But the soul has a mask too — it is more subtle and you will see it in the autumn time.

The soul mask is hidden from you because you are looking in another direction. You are looking for outcomes. The soul mask is operating when you think *if* you do something *then* something else will happen. When you are deciding on a strategy or simply thinking about what to do and the words *if* and *then* come into your thoughts you should realise that the mask to the soul is standing right behind you. The *if/then* rationale is, of course, the linear argument that hooks us in to expecting outcomes. To unmask yourself tell people what you want without explaining yourself. Express yourself without justifying why you are doing so. Be yourself without apology and don't give reasons for why you are who you are.

Summer time was the time for forging the steel. Now in the autumn you will test how well the forging process went. This is the final season in the development of your intuition. When you complete this season you will find that the seasons lose their meaning because they all overlap simultaneously. This is the multi-dimensional view of the seasonal model. It all happens in the same moment.

WORKSHOP

As autumn is a time of solitude it is fitting that you do these exercises alone and formulate your own rules of life from an intuitive perspective. This period is the experience and catalyst for an infinite array of possibilities for you that are yours alone.

EXERCISE ONE

INTUITIVE WRITING

There is a time to create, a time to rest, a time to work, a time to enjoy and a time to let go. All things end in the linear world. You can choose to view it as a death and mourn, or you can allow the winds of change to dance about your feet and celebrate.

Feelings of confusion. Failure to understand that change is here without knowing where it will lead. The trees become alive in death, displaying their inner glory through the colours in their leaves.

This is a time for colour. This is a time of statement. Statements that the harvest is finished. Statements that winter is coming. Statements that you are alive in raw beauty. Statement that the only time is now.

Experience the beauty of the present. Experience your glory. Externalise Externalise Externalise.

Autumn brings feelings of reverential awe, of deep knowing without understanding. A time to be profound, a time to feel your strength, a time to understand courage.

Contemplate the passage above. Tap into your intuition. If you are right-handed then use the left to write with; if you are left-handed then use the right to write with. Ask your soul to write a letter to you now.

MEDITATION

Find your meditative sanctuary.

Breathe in and relax as you exhale affirming:

I AM total trust
I AM total knowing
I AM love

Breathe in and relax as you exhale affirming:

I AM total trust
I AM total knowing
I AM love

Breathe in and relax as you exhale affirming:

I AM total trust
I AM total knowing
I AM love

Breathe in and relax as you exhale affirming

I AM total trust
I AM total knowing
I AM love

Now focus your attention on the inside of your head, right at the centre and see the colour indigo radiating out from this spot like a radio transmitter. Feel the indigo rays pulsating outwards transmitting the words to the universe.

I AM total trust. I AM total knowing. I AM love.

Stay in this meditation for approximately thirty minutes and on your return, choose your own closing affirmation, remembering to wrap yourself totally in golden light.

YOUR AFFIRMATION IS ....

EXERCISE TWO

INTUITIVE WRITING

In all business and indeed life there is a need to review past performance, no matter what the outcomes of our efforts have been. Be prepared for your evaluation now. When you choose to do this you will learn far more and increase your future successes infinitely.

There is beauty in the starkness. The tree stands naked, showing itself to the world as it is, as it was and where it is going. It is unashamed.

Silent, still power emanates from its stature. At this time there is no need for tinsel. There is no need for leaves. There is no need to beautify.

This is a time for you. Experience strength in openness. Experience the power of vulnerability. Experience the winds of change. Experience the beauty of who you are.

As life around you migrates to warmer climates, as you say your good-byes to the past, celebrate your oneness, be grateful for this time, free of anxiety and filled with love.

Contemplate the passage above. Tap into your intuition. If you are right-handed then use the left to write with; if you are left-handed then use the right to write with. Ask your soul to write a letter to you now evaluating your project as it stands.

MEDITATION

Focus your attention on your solar plexus. Relax as you breathe and affirm that:

I AM at peace with myself and the universe
I AM I AM I AM
I AM love now

Relax as you breathe and affirm that:

I AM at peace with myself and the universe
I AM I AM I AM
I AM love now

Relax as you breathe and affirm that:

I AM at peace with myself and the universe
I AM I AM I AM
I AM love now

Relax as you breathe and affirm that:

I AM at peace with myself and the universe
I AM I AM I AM
I AM love now.

Focus on your solar plexus and see it sending out rays of vibrant yellow light; feel the energy of enthusiasm; and hear the wisdom of evaluation.

Remain in this meditation focusing on this colour and part of your body for thirty minutes. On your return, choose your own closing affirmation remembering to wrap yourself totally in purple light.

YOUR AFFIRMATION IS: ....

EXERCISE THREE

INTUITIVE WRITING

It takes courage to release the past and it takes wisdom to integrate all that you have achieved. As your project winds down, know that new ideas are waiting to come to the surface, and know that they will be better than before. So dream now and search for new projects.

As the days continue to shorten, feelings of melancholy stir within, at the heart, at the very core of the soul.

A strangeness, feelings of sadness, a reluctance to let go of the last vestiges of all that was learnt and loved from the seasons through which you have passed in this cycle of your eternity.

It takes courage to release the past. It takes wisdom to integrate all that is learnt. It takes deep inner trust to acknowledge that all learning, all experience will lodge in the library of the soul for all time.

For in death there is life. In desolation there is hope. In release there is power. In life there is love.

Contemplate the passage above. Tap into your intuition. Once again, if you are right-handed then use the left to write with; if you are left-handed then use the right to write with. Ask your soul to write a letter to you now telling you about your next project.

MEDITATION

Focus on the point between your eyes and wrap it up in indigo light.

For thirty minutes meditate on the following:

In each season and each part of each season, there is total wisdom, knowledge, love, beauty, potential and complete growth that is you. You are perfect being you, where you are, and whom you represent.

As the autumn ends and you head towards the next beginning, your understanding of courage, patience, faith and your knowing increases. I AM WHO I AM BECAUSE I AM.

After the meditation list everything that you have learnt from your intuition since you started reading this book. Then ask your soul to tell you about your life's purpose. Write it down and frame it.

SUMMARY

1   Words are linear. They have meaning, definition and judgement attached to them. They build the frame of reference which allows us to communicate with others.

2 The soul is non-restrictive. It speaks a language where words are not necessary.

3 In the autumn time of your development you need to choose whether you wish to be one with you soul or remain permanently in the linear dimension.

4 It takes courage to be intuitive because living intuitively requires you to live now and nowhere else.

5 In this phase of your development you will learn how to relate to people differently.

6 Autumn is the time to know who you are.

7 When you are deciding on a strategy or simply thinking about what to do and the words of another come into your thoughts: know that the soul mask is standing right behind you.

15

In Search of a Higher Platform

My intuition is me
I am my intuition
We are one
We are the universe

My intuition is the universal bridge to unconditional love
My intuition is perfect love
I am perfect love
I am the universe

All inspiration comes via my intuition
All creativity rises intuitively
I am one with my intuition
I am inspirational
I am perfectly creative

My ears, my eyes, my touch all sense the diversity of the
universe
This is my personality, this is my aloneness
My heart senses love, my heart knows of unity
This is our soul, this is my oneness, this is my intuitive
power
My intuition is the way to understand my brothers and
sisters
It is the perfect communicator between us

My intuition speaks without language and is perfectly understood
My intuition perceives without hearing and comprehends perfect meaning
My intuition is expressionless yet its force is more powerful than the strongest wind.

I find my intuition in the silence
I find it in the ether
And I discover that my intuition is me

So how do I develop my intuition? By simply developing me.

AUTUMN IS A time unlike any other. It is a time of mixed feel-ings and of strange emotions that seem to have little bearing on our way of life. It is the time of integration. Inte-gration of the learning stimulated by the experiences of the seasons into the soul. Autumn in the linear perspective is the end of the seasonal cycles. Yet as we observe the seasons we note that they continue in perpetuity and so we see the futility of the linear myth.

As we search for higher, more challenging diving platforms, and we allow our intuition to lead us in these quests, we find that our vocabulary changes as does our perspective of linear reality. It is linear illusion to view any event as being a part of a cyclical trend. At the outset of this book I made it clear that we were using the illusion of sequential activity as a model from which to learn. Now that we are consciously intuitive and have chosen to live in the multi-dimensional world of total possi-bility, we need to recognise yet another reality.

This new reality has no dimension because it is infinite. It occupies no space because it is ever expanding. Every moment in which we live contains everything that we know as our reality, which after all is only one. We talk of progression. We talk of growth. We talk of concepts that have movement in them. Yet to achieve growth and movement we are required to find the stillness, the timelessness of the universe.

Multi-dimensional reality means there is no time; there is no continuum; there just is! Forever and forever and forever which is the absolute moment of now. In the multi-dimensional world of the soul there is no past; there is no future; there is only timelessness and in this timelessness there is absolute possi-bility forever and beyond. You are now in a world where intuition is the language.

You are the one who can find the door opening into the soul itself. This is the quest for the holy grail. This is the search for meaning and once found will take you beyond forever.

16

Questions and Answers

Everyone has questions about intuition. The questions listed below are the ones most frequently asked by reporters, journalists and television presenters. My responses are verbatim.

QUESTION: What is intuition? We talk a lot about women's intuition — is that what it is about?

ANSWER:Yes, in a sense it is. Intuition is frequently described as a woman's feelings because it has a feminine vibration to it. This energy is not sexual; it refers to the feminine essence that is within us all. Whether male or female we have both male and female energies running through us. A friend of mine says that she is a woman solely because she has two per cent more feminine energy than masculine energy. For men it is vice versa. Intuition, we all have it. What I have discovered since talking about intuition is that, because I am a male, men continually confide in me that they too use their intuition. A recent survey of male achievers asked this question about the use of intuition in making business decisions. Of the men questioned ninety-five per cent admitted that they went with their gut instinct in the final analysis. When asked if they spoke about it to their colleagues about the same percentage said no.

Q   *Do men suppress their intuition?*
A   Personally I don't believe men do suppress their intuition. I do think that they are frightened to admit it. They call it a gut instinct because they somehow believe that it is a sign of weakness to express their feelings. But part of expressing who you are is expressing your feelings. Western men have been brought up in an environment that teaches them not to feel. Men have got this block to get over.

Q   *Do you think more men are changing now and expressing their feelings and intuition?*
A   It is definitely changing. The number of people that come up to me after my lectures and acknowledge their intuition is always increasing.

Q   *Intuition is considered a lazy way to make decisions in some circles isn't it?*
A   Yes, it is. Usually by people who believe that life has to be hard to be worthwhile. When I get this question I always ask the audience to think of a time they experienced a gut feeling that they didn't act on and wished that they had. That's the proof of intuition.

Q   *Is that what intuition is — a gut feeling?*
A   Intuition is a knowing. You just know it. It is as simple as that.

Q   *Is there a scientific explanation for intuition?*

A   I haven't found one. Science first would need to define intuition and in doing so would limit it and make it untestable. We can all believe what we want to believe. I was at a sceptic meeting some time back and was asked to scientifically prove intuition. My response was to ask them to scientifically prove that scepticism was valid. Your proof in the linear world depends on which ideological stance we take. The discipline of logic says that first we must define the world that we are referring to and if something falls outside of that world then it is illogical. Intuition falls outside of the scientific model so it is unscientific. Science falls outside of the intuitive model so it is non-intuitive. Both are valid and real yet comparison is silly. The proof of intuition is in the results which are created by intuitive feelings and intuitive thoughts. So what I suggest to people is that they run their own scientific tests — intuitively.

Q   *How did you become intuitive?*

A   I went on a search for myself. Like many people, I wasn't happy with who I was so I threw everything up in the air. I decided that I wouldn't believe anything that anyone told me and went on my search for my truth. I started some personal growth courses and found that the more I became in touch with myself the more I worked intuitively. It developed from there to the point that I began working psychically on top of my intuition.

Q   *What do you mean by that?*

A   I found that at dinner parties, work functions and other gatherings I was starting to give future predictions. Much to my surprise and the surprise of others, they came true.

Q   *Did you use your intuition to predict things?*

A   Yes.

Q   *So you're not talking about fortune telling or anything like that?*

A   No, I'm not. I get a sense about people and am able to tell them something about themselves. That is quite different from fortune telling. Intuition is relevant to everyday life. It is relevant to what you are doing now. Intuition can look inside a person and predict on the law of probability an outcome.

Q   *Can you give us an example?*

A   When I was selling computer software I could go into any company and know where the business opportunities were. How does a mother know when her child needs her? Have you ever gone to pick up the telephone just before it rings? I could go on but I think you've got the message.

Q   *When speaking about intuition are we trying to define the spiritual?*

A   It definitely comes into it. You can't be intuitive unless you know who you are and understand that there is a greater wisdom inside and outside yourself. When people develop intuitively they go on a search to find out about the purpose of life and to know who they are. That's spiritual. That way they can distinguish between an ego desire and an intuition.

Q   *Do crises help us to develop intuitively?*

A   Life throws up to us crises so that we can dig deep down inside ourselves to find out just what we can do. That we can create prosperity and happiness in our lives is a fact of life. Often when the chips are down and a person has nowhere to go except inside themselves that is when they discover their own innate god nature. You only need to look at the number of millionaires that have been bankrupt to see the point.

Q   *What do you mean by prosperity?*

A   Prosperity is a lot more than having a million dollars in the bank. It is finding your life's purpose, feeling fulfilled and experiencing life with a passion. And to be able to recognise the qualities of life — that is living life to the full and being aware of life at all times. Ultimately every experience, even some that we might like to avoid, will enable us to learn and grow. We need to face our experiences head on. It takes courage to work in an intuitive sense because of that.

Q   *How do personality types as defined by personality profile tests relate to intuition?*

A   I believe that the characteristics defined in these tests describe how we express our intuition. Intuition runs through all categories of people. The way that they express themselves intuitively is through their personality type.

Q   *Is there one primary thing that we can do to enhance our intuition?*

A   Yes, you must recognise that you are intuitive and follow it. It is as simple as that.

Q   *Why do you think people are scared of intuition?*

A   I think because they feel that it will change their lives and that frightens them. People are often frightened to show their emotions in society because our society is not structured to allow them to do it.

Q   *Are science and intuition compatible?*

A   It is a matter of order. I would say that science is superb for scientific pursuits. We are created and born with an intellect. When we have an intuitive thought we can overlay it with intellectual reason. When we use our intuition this way it becomes a very powerful dynamic.

Q   *Children are intuitive. Why aren't they as intuitive as they get older?*

A   Think back to a time when your child embarrassed you when they were young. The chances are that he/she was acting from intuition and the innocent truth shocked you. Now think about your response. The chances are that you chastised them for being cheeky. The point that I am making is that we are all educated away from intuition. Our society does it, our education systems do and sadly we as parents do it. We are all so hung up on conformity and control that we take away the persona power of expression in the child. With it goes the intuition. It's like throwing the baby out with the bathwater.

Q   *What are the major do's and don'ts in developing intuition?*

A   Do use your intuition for your own well being. When you have an intuition do act on it. Do have fun with your intuition. Don't use your intuition to invade the privacy of others or to manipulate outcomes.

INDEX

action
   develops intuition 18–20
affirmations 36, 39, 58, 59, 67, 71,
      72, 83, 91, 99, 111, 117, 132,
      139, 146, 154, 156
aggressive behaviour 22
autumn 149–161
   defined 150, 161

belief patterns 51
beliefs
   function of ego 66
   linear 106
   purpose 66
   restrictive *50*
business
   need for effective planning 22

cause and effect 12, 65
change 76
choice
   intuitive 136
clearing
   defined 63
confidence 81
creative expression 90

deficit need 128
detachment

process of 66
   purpose of 66
disease 97

ego 17–27, 47
   blocks 47, *51*
   defined 21, 47, 68
   drive 91
   drives your personality 21
   expression of soul 23, 26
   filter *21*
   function 47, 68
   linear perspective 47–8
   position *49*
   role of 104
   survival mode 21–3, 26
ego statement vs intuition 77
enthusiasm 107–8
environment
   influences 18
expectations 129–130
   false 15
experiences
   growth 64
   purpose of 14, 63

false expectations 15
fear of death 14

flexibility 145
fulfilment 98

guardian angels 107

hunches 93

illusion of loss 14
imagination 116
impatience 34, 47
intellectual understanding 20
intuition
    as knowing 66, 115
    at work 49
    benefits 32
    blocks 51–5
    bridging realities 98
    characteristics 34
    coming of age 131
    creativity 23–4
    defined 67
    feelings 56
    function 47
    growth of 35
    imagination 44
    language of the soul 14, 18,
        107
    newly discovered 86
    potential 104
    predictive 79
    purpose 47
    recognition 55
    the seed 97, 98
    symbolism 55
    understanding it 81
    use of imagery 64
intuitive ability
    dormant 18
    innate 18
intuitive choice 136
intuitive development
    characteristics of 44
    initial stages 45
    support group 82

intuitive ethics 138
intuitive living
    courage 151
    experience 20
    inner process 45
    knowledge 20
intuitive logic 55
intuitive person 79
    traits 46
intuitive thought
    keeping records 25
    workshop 98

karma
    cause and effect 68
    old-karma 32

learning
    by experience 20
    through knowledge 20
linear beliefs 106
linear thinking 12
linear reality 114
    cause and effect 21
    defined 69
    ego filter *21*
    illusion of 65
    outcomes 96
love 104
    multi-dimensional 95
luck 25

meditation
    defined 56
    finding the silence 92
    initial experience 70
    ritual 93
    role of 70
    stillness 91
    use of 56
miracles 25
multi-dimensional reality 114
    creativity 97
    ego filter *21*

timeless 161
multi-dimensional thinking 13

needs
    defined 94
    model 95
negative beliefs 38, 59

optimism 144
outcomes 13, 151
    linear reality 96
    restrictive 97

past conditioning 34
person
    multi-dimensional 96
personal
    expression 94
    responsibility 15
personality 91
    influence of ego 21
    needy dependent 128
    types 109–110

questions and answers 163–7

random chance 25
release statement 71
results 96, 136

seasons
    as linear 31
    as multi-dimensional 31
    autumn 149–161
    role of 30
    spring 85–119
    start of cycle 30–1
    summer 121–147
    use of 30
    winter 29–84
social conditioning 18
soul
    as coach 83, 107

creative energy 90
    expression 87
    force 144
    growth 91
    mask 153
    traits of 105
soul-to-soul communication 18
spirit guides 107
spiritual growth 35–6
spirituality
    defined 90
    soul 90
spring 85–119
    role of 86, 88
    timing 96
    traits 86, 96
summer 121–147
    traits 125
suppressed beliefs
    release statement 71

thought
    as an impulse 37
    use of 47
thoughts
    creative 38
    healing 69
    power of 116

victim consciousness
    defined 67, 87

wants
    defined 94
    model 95
water 62
winter 29–84
    characteristics 35
    defined 31
    purpose of 67
    use of 31, 38

zeal 143, 144

FURTHER READING

Cairnes, M. *Peaceful Chaos — The Art of Leadership in a Time of Rapid Change*, The Change Dynamic, Sydney, 1992.

Campbell, J. *The Power of Myth*, Doubleday, New York, 1988.

Chopra, D. *Unconditional Life*, Bantam Books, New York, 1991.

Feist, E. *The Winning Edge*, Golden Spurs Publications, Sydney, 1989.

Johnston, R. *Owning Your Own Shadow*, Harper Collins, San Francisco, 1921.

Moore, T. *The Care of the Soul*, Harper Collins, San Francisco, 1992.

Ponder, C. *The Dynamic Laws of Prosperity*, DeVorss & Company, California, 1962.

Ponder, C. *The Healing Secrets of the Ages*, DeVorss & Company, California, 1967.

Wilson, P. *Instant Calm*, Penguin, Sydney, 1995.

Zukav, G. *The Seat of the Soul*, Random House, United Kingdom, 1990.

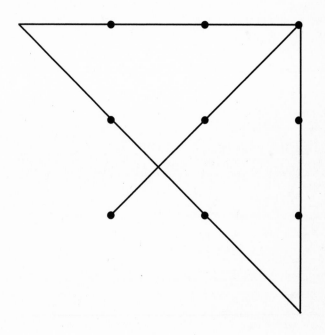